I0814137

HONEY CAKE & LATKES

RECIPES FROM THE OLD WORLD BY THE AUSCHWITZ-BIRKENAU SURVIVORS

HONEY CAKE & LATKES

RECIPES FROM THE OLD WORLD BY THE AUSCHWITZ-BIRKENAU SURVIVORS

AUSCHWITZ-BIRKENAU
MEMORIAL FOUNDATION

MELCHER
MEDIA

CONTENTS

FOREWORD BY RONALD S. LAUDER

The idea of an Auschwitz-inspired cookbook may appear, on the surface, to be a terrible joke or at least something in very bad taste. It's a complete juxtaposition, because the very word, *Auschwitz,* conjures up images of emaciated souls, starved, tortured, and murdered. To tie that into a book of recipes seems to make no sense.

But what you hold in your hands is quite the opposite. This book is a story of hope and triumph of the human spirit. As you turn the pages, I want you to keep something in mind. One of the most amazing and least-talked about stories from the Holocaust is one that nobody ever mentions: the people who survived, who walked out of that indescribable hell, walked with a rare determination to simply go on living. They never sought revenge; not one German was ever killed in retribution by a Jew after the war. These people lost everything—mothers, fathers, sisters, brothers, husbands, wives, and, in too many cases, their children—but they were determined to create new life. Surviving this unspeakable tragedy took the strength of character that most human beings cannot even imagine. And along with breathing, food is one of the chief components of life.

When I visited Poland for the 75th commemoration of the liberation of Auschwitz, on January 27, 2020, I had the extraordinary opportunity to talk with many of the 120 elderly survivors who made the trip back. Bringing the delegation of survivors to Auschwitz was a great privilege for me. But in our conversations, something very interesting came out. Of all things, we started talking about the recipes they brought back with them. They did this for a variety of reasons. It was a way of remembering a murdered mother or grandmother. It was a way to feed their children and grandchildren when food was and will always be precious to them. It was a way to hold on to the past and pass it down to our future. And, ultimately, it was so, so Jewish.

I remembered the wonderful dishes that my grandmothers made, and I compared these with them. Did they put sugar in their gefilte fish?

Survivors Tova Friedman, Angela Orosz-Richt, and Johnny Jablon, with Ambassador Ronald S. Lauder, photographed in Auschwitz-Birkenau on January 27, 2020, by Shahar Azran.

Were their honey cakes on the tart side? It's interesting that while the world knows my mother, Estée Lauder, as the founder of a cosmetics empire, her children and grandchildren remember her for her excellent matzo ball soup.

Food and aroma instantly bring back memories. Sometimes, memory is all that is left of the people we loved so dearly. This book has memory. It also has incredible recipes from some very special people. I hope you will take the time to use them in your kitchen. And when you put these beautiful dishes on the table, remember they are also served, as every Jewish mother serves everything she makes, with a large portion of love.

That, more than anything, is what has inspired this book.

A NOTE FROM THE EDITOR

More than a cookbook, what you are holding in your hands is a collection of heirloom recipes that convey survivors' stories through the mnemonic lens of cooking and food. We have tested and retested these recipes to make sure they can be replicated in your kitchen while keeping the original character and voice of the survivors who contributed to the volume.

In January 2020, the Auschwitz-Birkenau Memorial Foundation, under the leadership of Ambassador Ronald S. Lauder, brought 120 survivors to Auschwitz-Birkenau to commemorate the 75th anniversary of its liberation. Together with world leaders, dignitaries, and people of goodwill, we stood in front of the Birkenau "gate of death," on the grounds where survivors lost their families, childhoods, and innocence. United, we honored the memory of those who perished and celebrated the lives of those who survived.

Three months later, in the midst of the global lockdown, Ambassador Lauder reconvened the survivors who had traveled with us to Auschwitz. During Passover, he hosted the first of many bi-monthly online survivors' reunions organized by our Foundation. Acknowledging how hard 2020 was for survivors, many of whom were alone for the holidays, he asked everyone on the call to share their favorite gefilte fish and other Passover recipes.

As a result, we were inundated with recipes. Some were long and detailed; others were informally scribbled and incomplete. All of them captured something essential about each person, their family history, and their story through food. We spent the following months conducting multiple interviews with survivors and their families, weaving a unique tapestry of sensory tales of flavors and smells from the old world, accounts of loss and trauma, as well as heartwarming and poignant stories of new beginnings and healing. While working on the manuscript, thanks to the encouragement and help of Jo Carole Lauder, we also received a very special recipe shared by Marion Wiesel: Elie Wiesel's family latkes recipe that opens up the last chapter of this volume.

Finally, five of the survivors who contributed to this collection—Michael Bornstein, Lois Flamholz, Tova Friedman, Eugene Ginter, and David Marks—reunited at a special photoshoot in New York City, willing to represent the community of survivors in person. These contemporary photographs, alongside the vintage images that open this volume, connect the past with the present, creating a visual anchor for all of the recipes for honey cake, latkes, and everything in between.

Before cooking, we suggest you begin with reading the recipes' head-notes, as they are the heart and soul of this book. They hold all the memories that inspired this volume: from Eugene Ginter's recollections of the chocolate sandwich that his mother made to nourish and strengthen him after the liberation; the rakott krumpli recipe shared by Eva Shainblum, who recalls that this Hungarian dish of layered potatoes was the last meal she shared with her family before they were all deported to Auschwitz one day after Shavuot in 1944; Benjamin Lesser's vivid memories of his grandfather's orchard and gardens in prewar Munkatch, where every summer the family gathered to pick the fruit and make compote; family stories of Goldie Finkelstein's delicious and abundant cooking as a way to process the war trauma of scarcity, hunger, and depletion; to—finally—joyous memories of holiday meals shared by many survivors after the war with the second, third, and—now—the fourth generation. We hope that reading these extraordinary stories will fill your hearts with love and appreciation of traditions that unite and bring us comfort.

—Dr. Maria Zalewska, executive director of the Auschwitz-Birkenau Memorial Foundation

THE TABLE

One can imagine a table without a home. Somewhere in a garden, beneath a tree or a pergola. But the opposite, a home without a table, will no longer be a complete home.

The table is what joins us. Everyone can have their own room, bed, or desk, but a table remains communal. Each person can live in their own world—in school, in a yard, at work, in one's activities—but at mealtime, everyone comes together at the table. We set plates of food on the table, which tend most often to be of combined traditions, local colors, seasonal options, and selections from kitchens in far corners of the globe. Both guests and home dwellers meet at the table, so conversation resonates because the table is not just about a meal. The table reflects the rhythm of our life, the week's dynamic, the calendar of prayers and religious holidays, family discussions. The table is the most everyday cultural space.

In the camp, practically no one ate at a table. The culture was, after all, meant to disappear among the barely living prisoners. And with the disappearance of the prisoners was to disappear cultural memory, and within that, the culture of the table. A person did not survive alone—with this person survived nostalgia and memory, knowledge and feelings, traditions and customs . . . perhaps, at times, it would have been easier to survive alone, without all that baggage. It would then be a bit like a new birth. But that is impossible. This is, precisely, the core of survival.

And that is what this book is about—it is not only a collection of culinary recipes. It is a book about survivors' recipes, dishes, meals . . . about remembering the table, about the familial nature of food, about gatherings . . . about influences of traditions, conventions, and innovations in this cultural space, which centers—today, just as before—people around a table.

—Dr. Piotr M. A. Cywiński, director of the Auschwitz-Birkenau Museum

Left: Michael Bornstein's family buried this kiddush cup in the yard before they were deported to Auschwitz (for full story see page xviii).

Angela Orosz-Richt & family

ABOUT THE SURVIVORS

Eva & Ella Shainblum

Alexander Spilberg

Anneliese Nossbaum

Claire Heymann

David Lenga & family

Elisabeth & George Citrom

Sam & Frieda Weinreich

Eva Szepesi

Elie & Marion Wiesel

Eva Kerenyi

Tova Friedman

Eugene Ginter

Edith More

Goldie Finkelstein

David Marks

Irene Buchman & Olga Jaeger

Ruth Webber

Lea Roth

Rachel Roth

Benjamin Lesser & family

Max Garcia

Rosalie Simon

Lois Flamholz & family

Michael Bornstein & his mother

Vlad Munk

Miriam Ziegler

Eugene Ginter

David Marks & family

Rachel Roth & her husband, Shlomo

Eugene Ginter's grandparents, Avrum & Sara Chaim Obstfeld

Lois Flamholz & her husband, Sol

Angela Orosz-Richt & family

Eva Shainblum's brother David

Tova Friedman

Eva Szepesi

Goldie Finkelstein

Ruth Webber & family

Alex Spilberg

Rosalie Simon

Miriam Ziegler

MICHAEL BORNSTEIN

Michael Bornstein was born in 1940 in Żarki, Poland, to Sophie and Israel Bornstein. He had an older brother named Samuel. Michael's family led a happy life before the German occupation of Poland. Jews made up more than 50 percent of the town and were a thriving community. On July 11, 1944, Michael and his parents, brother, and grandparents were put on cattle cars and deported to Auschwitz. Upon arrival in the camp, men and women were separated. Michael, being four years old, was sent to the children's barrack. Soon after, Michael's mother learned that both Israel and Samuel were murdered in the gas chamber.

The children in Michael's barracks were older and took every opportunity to steal his bread. Sophie would sneak into the barracks to give him her bread rations. Even the beatings she received for her actions would not deter her. To further protect Michael, Sophie snuck him into the women's barracks, where his grandmother Dora would hide him under straw while the women went to work. When Sophie was sent to Austria to work in a munitions factory, Michael remained in the women's barracks with Dora. As the Soviet army advanced, the prisoners were set to embark on a death march. Neither Michael nor Dora would have survived the harsh conditions of the march. They hid in the infirmary, which saved their lives. After spending six months in the camp, Michael was liberated. When Sophie returned to Żarki, she searched for valuables they had buried in the backyard of their old house. Everything was stolen except for a kiddush cup that became a family heirloom.

In 1956, Michael and Sophie emigrated to the United States. Michael felt invisible in his new surroundings, where he didn't speak the language. He had no money, no father, and a number tattooed on his arm. Sophie taught Michael her optimistic mantra: "This too shall pass." That stayed with Michael for the rest of his life.

War experiences haunted Michael. He remembered the putrid smell of burning flesh, the sound of screams and marching boots, the beatings. As a result, he contemplated removing his tattoo and changing his name. After seven decades of silence, Michael recounted his story to his oldest grandson's classmates.

Michael lives in New Jersey with his wife, Judy. They have four kids and twelve grandkids. He still uses his mother's kiddush cup for every Shabbat, holiday, or special event as seen on page x.

IRENE BUCHMAN & OLGA JAEGER

Irene Buchman and Olga Jaeger were born in Bilke, Ukraine. In June 1944, Irene and Olga's family was taken to the Beregovo ghetto. Soon after, they arrived in the Nazi German concentration and extermination camp Auschwitz-Birkenau. The sisters were separated from their parents and brother but managed to remain together. As their mother stood in the selection line that would lead to her death, she instructed Irene, "Make sure you watch over Olga. Take care of her." Irene would spend the rest of her life making sure to fulfill that promise.

After a few grueling weeks, another selection took place. The kapos formed a circle around Olga. Irene was instructed to return to her barracks. An uneasy feeling told Irene that something was wrong. She grabbed Olga from the kapos' clutches and instructed her to run back to the barracks. Six other women followed suit. This would not be the last time that Irene would fulfill her mother's request. The two sisters were later transported to a munitions factory making bombs. On Yom Kippur, Irene was sent to the area in the munitions factory where bombs were sorted and packed. Out of respect and in honor of the day, she risked her life by carefully replacing active bombs with those she knew would not detonate.

In April 1945, the women were transported to Lübeck, Germany. Soon after arriving, they were forced to move from one location to the next as bombs rained from the sky, dropped by Allied planes. They were liberated by British soldiers. After liberation, Irene and Olga emigrated to the United States. Irene learned to sew and found a job in the garment district. In 1958, Irene went to Israel to visit her cousins and was set up on a blind date with the man who would become her husband. They got married and came to the United States, where they raised two daughters. Irene passed in February 2020, the month after her final visit to Auschwitz for the commemoration of the 75th Anniversary of its liberation. Olga lives with her family in New Jersey.

ELISABETH CITROM

Elisabeth Citrom was born in 1931 in Târgu Mureş, Romania. Her parents, Leopold and Malvina, raised Elisabeth and her brother, Isador, in a traditional Jewish home. Elisabeth's grandmother Bluma Salomon was a significant figure in her life. From 1940 the family experienced overt antisemitism, which Elisabeth felt from her teacher and classmates. Elisabeth's father was prohibited from practicing his profession. His former employees took over his legal practice. He was beaten and robbed. Elisabeth's house was seized, and the family moved to her grandmother's farm. The Hungarian Gendarmerie consisting of locals, carried out the government's anti-Jewish laws.

In late April 1944, the family was taken to the ghetto and placed in an old brick factory. They were taken to the station at the end of May to begin their journey to Auschwitz-Birkenau. It was the last time Elisabeth saw her mother and seventy-two-year-old grandmother. Elisabeth stayed in Auschwitz until November 1944 in the children's barracks. Her aunt, Yolanda Solomon, survived with her. Then they were taken to the labor camp Hamburg-Altona and subsequently to Lenzing, Austria. Americans liberated her on May 9, 1945. Her father and brother survived Bergen-Belsen and went to Sweden, but it took five years before they found each other.

Months after liberation, Elisabeth made her way to Israel. She served in the army, helped build a kibbutz, became an active member in a youth movement, studied and practiced nursing, and met her beloved husband, George, a fellow survivor. Elisabeth and George moved to Sweden and had two children, who had three children each. She currently lives in Israel. Elisabeth and George's son, Joel, is the vice-chairman of the Auschwitz-Birkenau Memorial Foundation.

GOLDIE FINKELSTEIN

Goldie Finkelstein was born in 1929 in Haifa, Palestine. The second of four children of Joseph and Miriam (Manya) Cukier, she grew up in Sosnowiec, Poland. She was ten years old when Nazis occupied her hometown and thirteen when Nazis grabbed her and her sister off the street to send them to a labor camp. Her father attempted to bribe the Nazis to release his daughters, but he was told, "Only one may go. You must choose!" With her father unable to choose, Goldie volunteered to stay. She was then sent alone to Graben, where women were forced to manufacture textiles for the Nazi military. Goldie survived a death march in 1945 from Graben to Bergen-Belsen, where she was liberated on April 15, 1945. She learned after liberation that in August 1943 her entire family had been deported to Auschwitz-Birkenau, where they were gassed and burned within hours of arrival. Goldie was left alone at fifteen years old, the sole survivor of her immediate and extended family. Goldie met Sol Finkelstein, an Auschwitz survivor, in a DP camp. The two married and emigrated to the United States, where they had three children. Sol passed in June 2013. Goldie passed in December 2019. Their son, Joe, sits on the board of the Auschwitz-Birkenau Memorial Foundation.

LOIS FLAMHOLZ

Lois Flamholz was born in 1927 in Zdenova, a small town in the Carpathian Mountains, Czechoslovakia. She was the oldest of four children, with two sisters and one brother.

Lois was deported to Auschwitz-Birkenau from the Munkács ghetto with her paternal grandparents, father's sister, and extended family. All were exterminated except for four cousins. Lois and her cousins were fortunate and remained together throughout their time in the concentration camps. Three out of Lois's four cousins survived the war.

After Lois and her cousins were liberated from Bergen-Belsen, they moved to Sweden. Lois remained there for two and a half years. In 1948, with the help of her two uncles, Lois emigrated to the United States. She attended night school in the Bronx, where she met her husband. The two wed the same year and built a home and a family together. Lois currently lives in New Jersey.

TOVA FRIEDMAN

Tova Friedman was born in 1938 in Gdynia, Poland. Her family came from Tomaszów Mazowiecki, Poland, and returned there when the war broke out. Her father was shocked at the devastation of his town. The fifteen thousand Jews were cramped into six four-story buildings, unable to leave without special permission. Tova and her family lived with their grandparents and other families in tight quarters, with the children sleeping and eating under the table. Starvation, shootings, and deportation soon decreased the population. Those who managed to survive were packed into trains and shipped off to German Nazi labor camps. A handful of Jews were kept as the "cleanup squad." Tova held her mother's hand as her mother and father picked up corpses and brought them to a communal grave.

Their next destination was the Starachowice work camp, where Tova's parents worked at an ammunition factory while the children roamed the streets of the towns surrounding the camp, careful not to get shot by the armed soldiers. When it was time for the children's selection in the camp, Tova remained hidden and managed to go unnoticed. However, soon after, when Tova was five and a half years old, she and her family were sent to the Nazi German concentration and extermination camp Auschwitz-Birkenau. Upon arrival, her head was shaved, and she was tattooed. Tova survived hunger, disease, and a trip to the gas chamber. Her mother's ingenuity saved both their lives when they hid amongst corpses instead of leaving on a death march. Tova and her mother both lived to experience the liberation of Auschwitz by the Russians on January 27, 1945. Tova states that it was her mother's brutal honesty that helped her survive. Although she was just a child, she understood her circumstances and the cruel reality that stood before her.

Tova and her parents immigrated to the United States when she was twelve years old. She has shared her story with students and audiences at public and private schools, colleges, and places of worship, as well as prisons. Tova received a bachelor of arts degree in psychology from Brooklyn College, a master of arts in Black literature from City College of New York, and a master of arts in social work from Rutgers University. She taught at the Hebrew University in Jerusalem and was director of the Jewish Family Service of Somerset and Warren Counties. Tova is blessed with four children and eight grandchildren. She lives in New Jersey.

MAX GARCIA

Max Garcia was born in 1924 in Amsterdam, Holland. Max's younger sister and parents were deported and murdered by the Nazis. Max survived in hiding. In 1943, after months of hiding, Max was deported to Auschwitz-Birkenau. Max triumphantly survived five concentration camps, including Auschwitz, Mauthausen, and the Westerbork transit camp. The U.S. Army liberated him on May 6, 1945. Speaking both German and English, Max convinced the U.S. Army to recruit him to work in its post-war counterintelligence as a translator in Europe. In 1946, he emigrated to the United States, sponsored by a U.S. Army officer, and eventually he moved to San Francisco. Max fulfilled his dream of becoming an architect. He married his wife, Pat, and was a father of three children and a grandfather of five children. Max passed in January 2021. May his memory be a blessing.

EUGENE GINTER

Eugene Ginter was born in 1939 in Kraków, Poland. During the Nazi occupation of Poland, Eugene spent his time in the Płaszów ghetto and later Płaszów concentration camp, Gross-Rosen, Brünnlitz labor camp, and Auschwitz-Birkenau.

Eugene was liberated, from Auschwitz, on January 27, 1945, just twelve days shy of his sixth birthday. After a stay in a hospital he was moved to a Jewish orphanage. Miraculously, Eugene's mother, who was saved by Oskar Schindler, found Eugene in the orphanage. Together, they traveled to Czechoslovakia and then Austria, where he reunited with his father.

In 1950, Eugene and his family emigrated to the United States, where he eventually became a mechanical engineer. He has been married to his wife, Rachelle, for the past fifty years. They have one daughter and two grandchildren. Eugene and Rachelle live in New York.

CLAIRE HEYMANN

Claire Heymann was born in 1929 in Großheubach, Germany, one of five children in an observant Jewish family. As there were not many Jewish families in their area, they often traveled to Frankfurt to observe Shabbat and holidays. Claire and her siblings attended a school where they were taught by Catholic nuns until they were expelled for being Jewish. During Kristallnacht, Claire's home was ransacked, and many of the family's possessions were destroyed. The town's mayor arranged shelter for the family. They spent the night in the local jail in a nearby village. Claire's neighbors helped fix up their home so the family could return. Since Claire couldn't attend school, her parents sent Claire and one of her sisters to be nannies for Jewish families in Frankfurt. Eventually the Gestapo arrested them and sent them to Berlin as slave laborers for the company Siemens from 1941 to 1943.

Claire was in Auschwitz from 1943 until 1945. Despite beatings and inhumane conditions, she survived thanks to her ability to speak German, which allowed her to work in the camp. Out of Claire's siblings, only two survived. Claire lives in New York.

EVA KERENYI

Eva Kerenyi was born in 1931 in Debrecen, Hungary, the only child in a well-to-do family. Her father was a lawyer, and her mother was a doctor. Eva enjoyed the luxuries that life had to offer. At the age of twelve, her life changed forever when she and her family were deported to Auschwitz-Birkenau. Eva spent six torturous weeks in Auschwitz and saw atrocities to last several lifetimes. She later spent time in Ravensbrück, Berlin-Schönholz, and Berlin-Neukölln camps. Eva was liberated by the Soviet army while on a death march.

On September 7, 1945, Eva returned to Hungary, where she and her mother lived with her maternal grandparents. Unfortunately, her father and many other family members did not survive the war. Eva completed her nursing degree and worked as a nurse until October 1956, when the Hungarian Revolution broke out. She was forced to forgo her acceptance to medical school. Eva resettled in Halifax with her future husband, Norbert Kerenyi, a doctor. In 1972, Eva and her husband moved to Toronto, where she still lives today.

DAVID LENGA

In 1927, David Lenga was born into a large Orthodox Jewish family in Łódź, Poland. His parents, Abraham and Sarah Lenga, led a more modern orthodox lifestyle than his grandparents. David had a younger brother named Nathan. The first language the boys were exposed to and learned was Yiddish. It became the brothers' *mamma loshen*, or mother tongue.

David had a wonderful childhood. His father was a businessman and owner of a large tannery in the small town of Stryków (18 kilometers south of Łódź). By the time David was four years old, he had learned to speak Polish, thus becoming bilingual. Throughout his five years of public education, he was an A student. Because David had a great thirst for learning, he loved going to school. David's parents also sent him to a cheder, a Jewish religious school, where he got his Jewish education.

David and his brother, Nathan, grew up in a very loving and caring family. His parents adored their children but raised them with a firm hand yet a tender, loving heart. They imbued their children with life values so strong that they became their guiding compass later in life. David was always an outgoing boy and surrounded himself with many close friends. His loving parents took the boys every year on summer vacations in the countryside, where they frolicked, climbing fruit trees and enjoying the fresh fruit. This wonderful life came to an abrupt end on September 1, 1939.

David was only eleven years old when Hitler's army brutally overran and invaded Poland. His life then became a nightmare. What followed was persecution, brutality toward the Jewish people, separation of families, incarceration in ghettos, deportations to slave labor and concentration camps like Dachau and Kaufering, and exterminations in death centers like Auschwitz-Birkenau. David went through six years of living hell. He survived by the skin of his teeth and by sheer luck. The American army liberated David on May 5, 1945. He was only 17 years old. After liberation, David discovered that his beloved father had also survived, but they were the only two survivors out of their large extended family with close to one hundred members. David currently lives with his family in California.

BENJAMIN LESSER

Benjamin Lesser was born in 1928 in Kraków, Poland, into a Jewish, middle-class family. He had an older brother, Moishe, two older sisters, Lola and Goldie, and a younger brother, Naftali, whom they called Tuli. Ben's parents, Shaindel (Shari Siegel) and Lazar Leser, came from well-known Orthodox Jewish families. Ben's father owned a kosher wine and fruit syrup manufacturing business, and a chocolate factory.

Growing up, Ben lived in two separate homes depending on the season. During the school year, the family lived in Kraków. During the summer, they moved to Munkács to be with his mother's family.

Before Germany invaded Poland in September 1939, Ben's life was typical of life in middle-class families in the area. He practiced his religion, pursued an education, and participated in rich cultural life. Although they were aware of the antisemitism that existed throughout Europe at the time, the Lesser family had remained mainly unfazed by it.

In March 1941, Ben and his family left Kraków for Niepołomice. In 1942, they escaped to Bochnia. In November 1943, Ben and his brother Tuli reunited with family members in Budapest. In May 1944, Ben and his entire family were crowded into cattle cars for deportation to the Nazi German concentration and extermination camp Auschwitz-Birkenau.

In June, Ben was sent to a rock quarry labor camp in Durnhau. Ben and his cousin Isaac survived a death march to Buchenwald, then a death train ride to Dachau. They were liberated from Dachau in April 1945. Tragically, Isaac died in Ben's arms. Ben lost consciousness, waking up four months later in St. Ottilien Hospital in Germany. He joined a young Zionist group and moved to Feldafing, Germany. In December 1945, Ben was luckily reunited with his sister Lola, Lola's husband, Mechel, and his nephew, Heshi. The four shared an apartment in Munich.

On September 21, 1947, Ben immigrated to New York, where he attended night school. To make money, he peddled hosiery on Delancey Street. In 1949, Ben moved to Los Angeles, where he married Jean Singer. Ben and Jean welcomed their first daughter, and soon after, Ben became a U.S. citizen. The couple had two more daughters. The family eventually moved to Las Vegas, Nevada, where Ben still lives today.

Ben did not speak of his experiences until 1995, when he spoke at his grandson's school. Ben has devoted his life to Holocaust education. He founded the ZACHOR Holocaust Remembrance Foundation.

DAVID MARKS

David Marks was born in 1928 in Şimleu Silvaniei, Romania. He was the ninth child of twelve in an upper-middle-class family. His father was in the import-export business, and the family also owned a farm. The Germans annexed David's village as a gift to Hungary, and life for the Jews changed drastically. The town's Jewish families were loaded onto cattle trains and traveled for four days without food or water. David was fifteen years old.

The train arrived in Auschwitz on a Friday, and by the afternoon, thirty-five of David's family members were murdered by the Nazis in the gas chambers. David landed a job in the kitchen, peeling potatoes, which he stole to buy shoes for his four sisters when he discovered they were alive, having seen them through the fence as they daily pushed and pulled garbage and bodies in wagons. One thousand five hundred boys lived in small, confined barracks. When scarlet fever broke out, the SS inspected the boys three times a day and sent anyone showing signs of the illness to their death in the gas chambers. The Nazis took 650 surviving boys to a German labor camp where 22,000 prisoners built fighter aircraft in a factory. They were being forced to march to Dachau concentration camp for elimination when the American Fifth Army liberated them.

After liberation, David ended up in Italy with only the clothes on his back. He survived due to the kindness of the Italians he encountered. Eventually, David boarded a ship to Palestine with 1,400 other young survivors. Boarding the vessel would be the first step to fulfilling a pledge David and his family had made: if they were to survive, they would reunite in Palestine. Unfortunately, the British intercepted the ship and rerouted it to Cyprus, where David was imprisoned for two years. David was eventually able to reunite with immediate and extended family members. Miraculously, eight of David's eleven siblings survived the war.

David joined the newly established Israeli Navy's police force. After his service, David joined his brother and his wife in the United States, where he met his wife, Miriam. He created a successful custom-made furniture factory in New York that is still in operation. Miriam died of cancer in 1993. David married his second wife, Kathy, in 2021. He passed away in 2022. He is survived by Kathy, four children, ten grandchildren, and one great-granddaughter.

EDITH MORE

Edith More was born in 1928 in the small Hungarian village of Ács. As the Nazi invasion gave rise to antisemitism, her idyllic childhood with her younger sister, Zsuzsi, older brother, Lazlo, and her parents was shattered. Edith spoke of their final Shabbats together, lighting candles in the basement, and their last Passover before the Nazis invaded their tiny village. Her beloved brother was already relocated to the Jewish ghetto, but Edith, her little sister, mother, and father were taken to the ghetto in Komárom. They spent a few nights sleeping on the mud floor of a brick factory before they were loaded onto cattle cars and transported to Auschwitz-Birkenau. When they disembarked from the cattle car, the Nazis removed her grandmother and took away her walker. Young Edith told them her grandmother needed the walker, and the Nazis simply responded, "Not anymore." Edith never saw her father or grandparents again.

As the war drew to an end and the Nazis began to flee Auschwitz, they told Edith that she needed to leave and join the march. Still, Edith was defiant and refused to go because her mother was too sick to leave. The Nazis threatened to shoot everyone who stayed behind. As it turned out, the Nazis did not have time to come back and kill the remaining prisoners, and Edith and her mother were there for the liberation of Auschwitz. They remained there for months until her mother's health improved.

Returning home was not easy. Eventually, while in Budapest, Edith met her soon-to-be husband Ferenc. They married in 1950, had a daughter, Susie, in 1953, and fled to the United States during the 1956 revolution. They were given plane tickets to Australia, but Frank's cousin advised them to go to America. Once in America, they were rejected by Edith's uncle and his family in Buffalo, so they traveled to California to find Edith's aunt and cousin, who took them in and helped them get settled in Los Angeles. Edith worked odd jobs and eventually started her own business: a small dress shop in Santa Monica.

Edith and Frank had a surprisingly optimistic view about their new lives in Los Angeles. They raised their daughter, Susie, and a son, Erwin, born in 1958, and remained married until Frank died in 2009. Edith still lives in the home that she and Frank bought together and enjoys the company of her children, grandchildren, and great-grandchildren. Her recipes have become a family legacy.

VLAD MUNK

Vlad Munk was born in 1925 in Pardubice, Czechoslovakia. After the German occupation, in March 1939, Czechoslovakia became part of the Third Reich, and all the German anti-Jewish laws came into effect. On December 6, 1942, all Jews of Pardubice were deported to the Theresienstadt ghetto.

On October 1, 1944, Vlad and his father were deported to Auschwitz-Birkenau, followed by his mother's deportation on October 12. Vlad never saw his parents again. Vlad was sent from Auschwitz to a subcamp, Gleiwitz I, where prisoners repaired railroad rolling stock for the Reichsbahnausbesserungswerk Company. On January 18, the camp was evacuated, and Vlad was forced on a three-day march to Blechhammer concentration camp. Soviet soldiers liberated Vlad.

After liberation, Vlad moved to Prague and enrolled in the Technical University to study chemistry. He graduated in January 1950 with an M.S. in chemical engineering and, after three years of graduate studies, received a Ph.D. in biochemistry and microbiology. Vlad worked as a research scientist from 1953 until 1969 at several research institutes in Prague and published numerous scientific papers and patents. He was awarded the State Prize of the Czechoslovak Republic in May 1968.

Vlad accepted an invitation from the dean of science of SUNY Plattsburgh, joined the faculty, and eventually got tenure. He retired in 1990.

Vlad met his future wife, Kitty Lowi, in Theresienstadt, and they eventually reunited and married in November of 1949, five years after they met. Vlad and his wife had two sons, Peter and Paul.

ANNELIESE NOSSBAUM

Anneliese Nossbaum was born in 1929 in Guben, Germany. In 1935, she became painfully aware of her Jewish identity when the Nazis revoked her family's citizenship. She was no longer allowed in the public swimming pool and banned from attending public school. In November 1938, during Kristallnacht, Anneliese's synagogue was burned to the ground. As the daughter of the cantor, she considered the synagogue her second home. In July 1941, when she was twelve, Anneliese and her family were ordered to move to a cloister with 474 other people. They were later deported to Terezin in Czechoslovakia. In October 1944, she was deported with her mother to Auschwitz.

After five grueling days, Anneliese and her mother were again deported to an airplane factory in Freiberg, Germany, where she was forced to make airplane parts. She bartered a piece of bread for a soap dish and another for a comb. She could carry both with her until the liberation. In April 1945, she and her mother were deported to Austria's Mauthausen concentration camp in open cattle cars. In May, they were liberated by the American army. Anneliese's mother, afflicted with tuberculosis, died in a hospital in December 1945. Orphaned Anneliese moved to New York City in 1946.

Anneliese devoted herself to Holocaust remembrance. She was a lecturer who shared her experiences with more than 10,000 school students, private organizations, and governmental institutions. Anneliese had two children and was a beloved grandmother to four grandchildren. Anneliese passed in March 2020.

ANGELA OROSZ-RICHT

Angela Orosz-Richt was born in 1943 in the Auschwitz-Birkenau concentration camp.

In 1943, Angela's mother was deported from Hungary to Auschwitz while three months pregnant. Angela's mother made the difficult decision to keep her pregnancy a secret at the risk of being killed upon discovery. Angela was born on December 21 in Barrack C.

Right after giving birth, Angela's mother was ordered to stand at *Appell*, roll call, in the cold. Without even the slightest movement, she finished the roll call and returned to her newborn child. Miraculously, with the help of the other women in the barracks, Angela survived without being discovered. Angela's father was murdered, and she and her mother relocated to a displaced persons camp with 800 Holocaust survivors. Many doctors refused to take the challenge of nursing Angela back to health, but one courageous doctor helped. Angela's mother remarried a Holocaust survivor who tragically lost his wife and daughter. This meant that Angela gained a stepbrother.

Angela's family settled in Hungary. Angela married, became a teacher, and had her first child. In 1966 her mother escaped Hungary with the help of Angela's stepbrother. Angela fled Hungary in 1973 and relocated to Toronto, Canada. Her second child was born in 1982. She currently lives in Montreal, Canada.

RACHEL ROTH

Rachel Roth was born in 1925 in Warsaw, Poland, to Golda and Samuel Rothstein. She was the oldest of four children in a highly religious family. Her mother, Golda, owned a men's clothing store, and her father, Samuel, was a rabbi, writer, and journalist editor of the *Yiddishe Tugblatt*. Rachel enjoyed a happy childhood full of games and laughter.

Rachel was only thirteen when the Nazis invaded Poland. Soon after, Rachel and her family were transferred to the Warsaw ghetto, where life was riddled with violence, poverty, starvation, and death. Typhoid was rampant and tragically took the life of Rachel's grandfather. Raids and deportations became constant, and Rachel and her family hoped to remain hidden in a bunker. Rachel even smuggled guns into the ghetto on multiple occasions and was eventually smoked out of her bunker during the Warsaw ghetto uprising. Rachel and her remaining family members were deported to the Majdanek concentration and death camp.

One day, in Majdanek, Rachel was one of 700 women brought into a gas chamber and told that they would spend the night there until morning deportation to another camp. Rachel would later find out that an accounting error was discovered before they entered the gas chamber. Only five hundred women were scheduled to be gassed that evening. The transport that was intended to be deported was mistakenly switched with the transport designed to be killed. In a sense, this German "accounting error" had saved her life.

On July 8, 1943, Rachel arrived from Majdanek in Auschwitz. Upon arrival, prisoners shaved Rachel's hair and tattooed the number 48915 on her body. She and Hela were housed in a cramped barracks and were assigned the difficult task of breaking stones. Rachel was fortunate and eventually secured a job in the clothing chamber (Bekleidungskammer), sorting through piles of clothes, shoes, and belongings confiscated upon arrival in Auschwitz.

In November 1944, Rachel and Hela were transferred to Bergen-Belsen. They were liberated on April 15, 1945, by the British Army.

After liberation, Rachel traveled to Paris, where she waited for her papers to enter Palestine. Rachel married Shlomo and together they emigrated to the United States. They built a business and had five children. Rachel attended the 75th anniversary of the liberation of Auschwitz with three generations of the Roth family. She passed away in 2022.

LEA ROTH

Lea Roth was born in 1925 in Brustury, Czechoslovakia, the youngest of five children. Her mother died when she was just five years old. After her mother's passing, Lea's father remarried and had an additional five children. Due to a strained relationship with her stepmother, she left her childhood home at fourteen. Lea eventually found comfort in her cousin's house.

In December 1944, Lea moved to the Sekernice ghetto. In April 1944, the SS began liquidating the ghetto. Jews were instructed to pack food for at least three days. Lea and her cousins did as they were told, unaware that this was a mere ploy to keep them ignorant of what lay ahead. Lea promised her cousin that she would look out for her children. Unfortunately, it was a promise she would not be able to keep. Lea and her family were loaded into cattle cars and deported to Auschwitz. Upon arrival, she was separated from her cousins, who were killed that very day. Lea spent three excruciating months in Auschwitz. She was eighteen years old.

Later, Lea was transferred to Stutthof concentration camp. By coincidence, she ran into Tzipora, a young girl she knew from the ghetto. Being five years her elder, Lea instinctively took this young child under her wing. It was a friendship that would last a lifetime. Unfortunately, Lea was transferred to Braunau concentration camp, leaving her friend behind.

Lea spent one year in Braunau, forced to make bombs for the Germans. Lea was taken on a death march toward Germany. It was during this march that Lea found out that Germany had surrendered, and the war was over. Like most survivors, Lea made her way back home. Only her sister, Margit, survived.

Decades later, Lea, accompanied by her daughter, stood in the Miami Beach Holocaust Memorial, staring at a photograph of herself, depicting her departure from the ghetto to Auschwitz. It is this very moment that led to the title of her memoir, *My Eyes Looking Back at Me: Insight into a Survivor's Soul.*

Lea currently lives with her family in Monsey, New York. She has a son and daughter, eight grandchildren, and twelve great-grandchildren.

EVA SHAINBLUM

Eva Shainblum was born in the Transylvanian city of Oradea in 1927, while it was still a part of Romania. It came under Hungarian rule later and was renamed Nagyvárad. The Hungarians carried out most of the persecutions and deportations of Jews for the Nazis. Before World War II, Nagyvárad was a town with almost 30,000 Jewish residents.

Eva was then known to her family as Reizi. Her father, Bela Steinberger, was a wholesaler for the Rippner Comb Manufacturing Company. Though he wasn't religious, he became a ba'al teshuvah when he married Esther, née Rosenberg. Their love was a true romance story, childhood sweethearts who were kept apart for years by Esther's family, who worried that Bela would pull her from their Orthodox values. Eventually, the family relented; Bela and Esther married and had four children: Paul, David, Ella, and Reizi. The family struggled financially but had a happy and loving home.

The beginning of the end came in May 1944, when the Hungarian fascists forced all the Jews in Nagyvárad into a ghetto. Polish refugee Jews were rounded up first, and Bela risked his life to allow several Polish Jews to escape through his backyard. Later, the Hungarians rounded up all the men in the community and tortured them to locate their valuables. Hungarian gendarmes ripped Esther's wedding ring from her hand, but Reizi and Ella threw their watches—gifts from their parents—into the fireplace to keep them from the fascists.

Less than a month later, on the eve of Shavuot 1944, all Jewish residents of the city were loaded onto cattle cars and sent to Auschwitz. Because the war was already in its final stages, and Soviet and Allied troops were closing in, most Hungarian Jews, including almost all of Reizi's family, were immediately sent to the gas chambers. The Nazis murdered Reizi's brother Paul one day before liberation. Only Reizi and Ella survived Auschwitz and were later sent to Nazi labor camps, including Weisswasser in Czechoslovakia, where Soviet troops liberated them. They ended up walking most of the way back from Czechoslovakia to Romania, but tragically, Ella caught typhus and died not long after their return.

All alone, Reizi sold her family's home and belongings for a pittance and ended up in a displaced persons camp in Germany. She eventually made it to Montreal, Canada, via a program sponsored by the Canadian Jewish Congress. She later met and married Max Shainblum, and had two children, Esther and Mark, and two grandchildren, Maya and Noa.

ROSALIE SIMON

Rosalie Simon was born in 1931 in Kriva Velka, Czechoslovakia, the youngest of six children: five girls and one boy. At eleven, Rosalie was expelled from school because she was Jewish and forced to wear a yellow star and abide by a curfew. On Passover of 1944, she and her family were ordered to pack up their essential belongings and deported to a ghetto in Hungary. After six weeks in the ghetto, the Nazis loaded Rosalie and her family onto cattle trains, where she was separated from her family and crammed into another car. When the train finally stopped, they saw smoke pouring out of chimneys and heard screaming SS and barking dogs. Rosalie was reunited with her family, and a selection began. Trucks were waiting for those too ill or weak to walk. The SS guards sent mothers with babies, young children, and the elderly to the left. The others were shunted to the right.

At the ages of twelve and forty-five, respectively, neither Rosalie nor her mother was deemed qualified for labor. They were sent to the left together, to their imminent death in the gas chambers. Her father, four sisters, and thirteen-year-old brother were sent to the right. Rosalie was devastated by her separation from her sisters. She left her mother without a word, hoping to find her sisters and bring them back to join her mother. Although she was successful in finding her sisters, they were unable to return to their mother. She was marching to her death in the gas chambers alone. Rosalie found out later that her brother was taken from her father and suffered the same gruesome fate.

Other prisoners shaved Rosalie's hair and disinfected her body. She received a striped dress and walked to her assigned barracks. She quickly learned that questions were not allowed in Auschwitz and that she had entered hell on earth. Rosalie accepted her fate. As long as she had her sisters, she was not alone. One day, her barracks was selected to go to Germany for labor. The train arrived at Geislingen, where they worked in the munitions factory. As the war was nearing an end, the women were transferred to Allach, a subcamp of Dachau, where they were starved almost to death. Rosalie found herself on a train once again. The train stopped in the middle of a field, where the American army liberated them. Helen, Charlotte, Lenka, Rajzi, and Rosalie survived together.

Rosalie has dedicated herself to teaching others, believing she is the voice for all those silenced by the Nazis. She currently lives in New York.

ALEXANDER SPILBERG

Alexander Spilberg was born in 1930 in Transylvania, Romania, the oldest of five children in a poor religious family. In 1941, the Hungarians took control of Transylvania and gradually restricted Jews' education and businesses. Life for Alex's family became even more complicated in 1942, when his father was deported to a forced labor camp. The family's financial strain intensified, and Alex often went to bed hungry.

In spring 1944, Jews were rounded up and taken to the Kolozsvár ghetto. In April 1944, they were packed into cattle cars in unbearable conditions. The trains had little ventilation and were packed so tightly that movement was nearly impossible. They traveled for four excruciating days without food, water, or the faintest idea of their destination.

When the train reached Auschwitz, SS soldiers instructed all Jews to leave their belongings and line up. Selection took place, with some ordered to go left and others sent to the right, unaware that this decision would seal their fate. Anyone deemed unfit for slave labor would be sent to their cruel death in the gas chambers. Arrival at the camp would be the last time Alex would see his mother, brothers, and grandparents.

When Alex arrived at his barracks, prisoners informed him that this was an extermination camp. Alex witnessed extreme cruelty. He remained in the camp until the winter of 1945. Toward the end of his stay in Auschwitz, the prisoners heard explosions, sparking hopes of liberation in the distance. Instead of being liberated, the prisoners were sent on a death march. They marched in the bitter cold and eventually arrived at Mauthausen concentration camp. Alex remained in Mauthausen for two months, until he was sent on another death march. Those who survived the six-day march arrived at Mauthausen subcamp Gunskirchen. Alex was liberated from Gunskirchen on May 4, 1945.

Alex returned home after liberation, but nothing remained of the life he once knew. Lack of paperwork forced Alex to emigrate to Canada instead of the United States, where he initially intended to go. Alex met his wife, Sarah, and had four daughters. After Sarah passed, Alex married his second wife, Miriam, who had three children. Together, they have sixteen grandchildren. Alex was the sole survivor of his family. Alex currently lives with his family in Ontario, Canada.

EVA SZEPESI

Eva Szepesi was born in 1932 in Budapest, Hungary. In 1942, like all Jewish men, her father was forced to join the Hungarian labor service. In April of 1944, after the Germans had occupied Hungary, Eva's mother sent Eva and her aunt to flee to Slovakia. Eva was eleven at the time. Her mother promised that she would follow them with Eva's seven-year-old brother, Tamas, as soon as she could. Once in Slovakia, Eva's aunt left her behind, and several different families hid Eva until the Nazis captured her in September 1944.

In mid-October 1944, she was brought to the Sered' concentration camp by cattle car and then deported to the Nazi German concentration and extermination camp Auschwitz-Birkenau. On November 3, 1944, Eva arrived in Auschwitz-Birkenau. After a horrific period and barely alive, she was liberated by the Russian Army on January 27, 1945. The Red Cross cared for Eva, and on September 18, 1945, she returned to Budapest, where she found her uncle and aunt, who then raised her.

Eva trained to be a seamstress and, in 1951, married Andor Szepesi. In 1952, she gave birth to their first daughter, Judith. In 1954, her husband received an offer to work in Frankfurt am Main, Germany. Two years later they were on a brief vacation back in Budapest when the Hungarian Revolution of 1956 broke out. Family friends in Frankfurt applied for refugee status on their behalf and they were able to return to Frankfurt, where Eva still lives. In 1964, they welcomed their second daughter, Anita. Eva and her husband, a furrier by trade, worked together in their fur boutique until he passed away in 1993. In 1995, she visited Auschwitz with her daughters to commemorate the fiftieth anniversary of the camp's liberation. Eva was inspired to break her silence and began to tell her story. She continues to go to schools to tell her story in honor of those who can no longer speak for themselves. Eva has two daughters, four grandchildren, and three great-grandchildren.

RUTH WEBBER

In 1935, Ruth Webber was born into a traditional Jewish family in Ostrowiec, Poland. Her father was a photographer who owned a photography studio. Ruth's grandmother also lived with the family. Her other grandparents and family members lived only a few doors away, allowing the family to gather every Shabbat. Ruth's grandfather was a cantor in the town.

Ruth was four when the Germans invaded Poland in 1939. The happy childhood Ruth was accustomed to drastically changed. The family lived in a constant state of anguish and fear. On one occasion, Ruth saw her grandfather crying. The German soldiers had cut off his beard. In 1940, the Nazis formed the Ostrowiec ghetto, which encompassed Ruth's home. Although they could remain in their home, other family members would share the living space. Ruth's sister, a pianist, returned from her conservatory in Warsaw to the ghetto. Her extraordinary talent even caught the eye of SS officers, who would come to the ghetto to hear her play. Arrangements were made for her sister, Helen, to disguise her identity and live with a family outside the ghetto. Ruth's parents suggested the same to Ruth, but she declined to leave and remained with her family. Her grandparents and other family members were on the first transport to Treblinka and never heard from again.

After moving between five different ghettos and work camps, Ruth and her mother were sent to Auschwitz in August 1944. In October 1944, her mother was transferred, leaving Ruth alone and devastated. While in the children's barracks, someone told Ruth that her father was alive and arranged for the two to meet. Ruth saw her father through a fence. He wanted to help and threw over cigarettes so she could trade them for food. Ruth was able to see her father several times. Her father did not survive the war.

Ruth was liberated from Auschwitz on January 27, 1945. She and the other surviving children were placed in an orphanage in Kraków. Having already found her sister, Helen, Ruth's mother tracked down Ruth and put them both in a children's home in Bielsko-Biala for safety. The three escaped to Munich and immigrated to Toronto two years later to live with distant relatives. Ruth's father and thirty-five family members perished. Ruth married Mark Webber in 1956 and moved to Detroit, where she had three children and five grandchildren.

ELIE WIESEL

Elie Wiesel was born in 1928 in Sighet, Transylvania, now a part of Romania. He was fifteen years old when the Nazis deported him and his family to Auschwitz. His mother and younger sister perished; his two older sisters survived.

Elie and his father were later transported to Buchenwald, where his father died shortly before the camp was liberated in April 1945.

After the war, Elie studied in Paris and later became a journalist. During an interview with the distinguished French writer François Mauriac, he was persuaded to write about his experiences in the death camps. The result was his internationally acclaimed memoir, *La Nuit* or *Night*, which has since been translated into more than thirty languages.

In 1978, President Jimmy Carter appointed Elie chairman of the President's Commission on the Holocaust. In 1980 he became the founding chairman of the United States Holocaust Memorial Council.

He is also the founding president of the Paris-based Universal Academy of Cultures. Elie has received over one hundred honorary degrees from institutions of higher learning.

A devoted supporter of Israel, Elie also defended the cause of Soviet Jews, Nicaragua's Miskito Indians, Argentina's desaparecidos, Cambodian refugees, the Kurds, victims of famine in Africa, victims of apartheid in South Africa, and victims of war in the former Yugoslavia.

Teaching was always central to Elie's work. In 1976, he became the Andrew W. Mellon Professor in the Humanities at Boston University, where he also held the title of university professor.

He is the author of more than sixty books of fiction and non-fiction.

For his literary and human rights activities, he received numerous awards, including the Presidential Medal of Freedom, the U.S. Congressional Gold Medal, and the Medal of Liberty Award, and the rank of Grand Officer in the French Legion of Honor. In 1986, Elie Wiesel won the Nobel Prize for Peace. A few months later, Marion and Elie Wiesel established the Elie Wiesel Foundation for Humanity. Professor Elie Wiesel passed away in New York City on July 2, 2016. May his memory be a blessing.

SAM WEINREICH

Sam Weinreich was born in 1919 in Łódź, Poland. He was the sixth of nine children, five boys, and four girls. Sam's father and all his married siblings worked in the furniture business. Sam's father prayed in a religious shtiebel. Sam was a member of the synagogue choir, singing at one of the most famous synagogues in Łódź for many years.

At the beginning of 1940, a decree was issued that Jews must abandon their homes and businesses and move into the Łódź ghetto. Two of Sam's married brothers and their families moved in with them. Surviving in the ghetto depended on being useful in some way. Sam's experience in the furniture business allowed him to work in a furniture finishing shop.

In 1944, the Germans claimed that everyone in the ghetto would be moving to a new location to work in better conditions. Sam's mother and several siblings had already died from hunger in the ghetto. Sam's father felt he was too old to travel, so Sam's sister decided to stay behind with their father. Sam put on his best suit and walked to the train, where he received a loaf of bread and some honey. He was then put in a cattle car headed to Auschwitz-Birkenau.

When the transport arrived in Auschwitz, Sam was sent right, which meant averting immediate death in the gas chambers. He was sent to a barracks to strip and his head shaved. He was then sent to take a shower. Wet and naked, the prisoners ran to another building, where each received a jacket and a pair of pants. Sam's coat had a number on it, which became his new identity. The following day, everyone stood in line to receive a bowl of soup that was passed around. To dehumanize the prisoners, they were not given spoons, forcing them to sip the liquid, like dogs. By the time the bowl reached the last person, there was none left.

Three days after arriving in Auschwitz, Sam was sent to Kaufering, a system of eleven subcamps of the Dachau concentration camp. After liberation, Sam went to live in a displaced persons camp in Landsberg, Germany where he met his future wife, Frieda Gola. They married on September 3, 1946, and celebrated their seventy-third anniversary on the same day that Sam celebrated his 100th birthday. They still live in Memphis, are active in the community, and speak about their experiences during the Holocaust in schools and other venues around the city.

FRIEDA WEINREICH

Frieda Weinreich was born in 1924 in Łódź, Poland, in an observant and loving household. She was the youngest of six children. She enjoyed a normal and happy childhood in Łódź, where she attended a Jewish all-girls public school and dreamed of studying accounting. Then, only months after her fifteenth birthday, the security she had known was shattered, as the Nazis invaded Poland. Her neighborhood in Łódź, which boasted a large thriving Jewish community, was transformed into the Łódź ghetto.

In August of 1944, as the Soviet troops advanced, the Łódź ghetto was liquidated by the Nazis. Along with her mother and the other Jews of the ghetto, Frieda was transported to Auschwitz-Birkenau. Upon their arrival, they were greeted by Dr. Joseph Mengele, who determined the fate of those who arrived in the camp. Frieda's mother was sent to the left. Not knowing what this fate meant, Frieda pleaded with Dr. Mengele to stay with her mother. However, before Dr. Mengele had a chance to decide her fate, a couple of prisoners pulled Frieda away from her mother, sending her to the right. That was the last time she ever saw her mother. She never had the chance to learn the names of her fellow prisoners, but Frieda insists they were two angels who saved her life.

Fortunately, Frieda spent only three days in Auschwitz-Birkenau before being transported to the Kristianstad labor camp, close to Berlin. Shortly after, Frieda learned she was included on a list of twenty girls going to another Nazi German labor camp in Czechoslovakia called Parschnitz. There, quality of life drastically improved. Frieda worked in a factory that produced gas masks.

In January of 1945, Frieda was liberated and made her way back to Poland in search of any living family. When she learned there were no other survivors among her immediate family, she didn't stay in Poland. She arrived at a displaced persons camp in Landsberg, where she met her future husband, Sam Weinreich. As the sole survivors of their families, they married in September of 1946 and began to rebuild their lives.

In 1949, Sam and Frieda received their papers to leave for America. They settled in Memphis, Tennessee, where they landed due to Sam's background in the furniture finishing industry. Seventy years after arriving in Memphis and having built a beautiful life and family there, Frieda and Sam remain active Jewish community members. They are among the city's very last few Holocaust survivors.

MIRIAM ZIEGLER

Miriam Ziegler was born in 1935 in Radom, Poland, to Rose and Hershel Friedman. She was an only child in a well-to-do family that owned and operated several clothing and general goods stores.

In 1939, Miriam and her mother traveled from Radom to Ostrowiec to find a hiding place to escape the Nazis. They heard German soldiers shooting in the distance and hid in the bushes as the Nazis killed the driver. In exchange for money, a Polish farmer allowed Miriam and her mother to hide temporarily. Later, as the danger for Jews was intensifying, Miriam's parents smuggled her into the Ostrowiec working camp with them. In 1944, all those working in the camp were loaded onto cattle trains and deported to Auschwitz.

Upon arrival in Auschwitz, Miriam was separated from her parents and the rest of her family. Their arrival at the camp would mark the last time Miriam would see her father. Miriam's head was shaved, and she received a tattoo with the number A1689. She was placed in the same barracks as children who were used for horrid pseudo-scientific experiments. Miriam was liberated from Auschwitz on January 27, 1945.

After Miriam's liberation from Auschwitz, she and other children were sent to a Kraków orphanage. Miriam left a note in the Kraków train station with her name and her parents' and grandparents' names in the hopes that they would find her, unsure of who was still alive. An old friend from her hometown came across the note and informed Miriam's mother, Rose, who was in Czechoslovakia, with Miriam's aunt, Bella. When Rose and Bella came to the orphanage to reunite with Miriam, she told them that she had seen her grandmother Faiga in Auschwitz and believed she might still be alive. Rose, Bella, and Miriam traveled to Ostrowiec in search of Faiga. They were lucky and found her.

Miriam, Rosa, Bella, and Faiga ended up in a displaced persons camp, Linz-Bindermichl. Although Rose opened a kiosk selling newspapers and cigarettes, she could not afford to support all of them. Miriam was sent to an orphanage in the Austrian mountains, where she learned Hebrew and math. She found comfort in nature and returned to good health.

Meanwhile, Canada agreed to let 1,000 Jewish orphans in, and in 1948, Miriam, her mom, and aunt moved to Toronto. Her grandmother joined them soon after. In 1957, she went on a blind date with survivor Roman Ziegler. They married in 1958 and had three children and four grandkids.

BREAKFAST *and* BRUNCH

ארוחת בוקר ובראנץ'

CHOCOLATE SANDWICH

Survivor | **EUGENE GINTER**

I will share with you a recipe for a chocolate sandwich that my mother made for me right after the war when we lived in Germany. She used this recipe to fatten me up.

My mother used to say, "I'd rather spend the money on the butcher than the doctor." After the war, things were tight. I had pictures of me where the biggest object on my face was my ears. I looked like Dumbo with the ears. I was so skinny, very emaciated. I had these gigantic ears and a small face, and I didn't like food. If I saw a lot of food, I would throw up, I guess from the hunger. . . . When my mother found me after the war, she tried certain things. I would only eat certain things. I liked chocolate. Who doesn't? She would take a slice of black bread, put a lot of butter on it, then take hard chocolate and shave it down and pat it into the butter. She was trying to fatten me up. So, I would bite into this thing. How bad can black bread be with butter and chocolate?

SERVES 1

1 slice black bread
1 tablespoon butter
1 block of dark chocolate

On a slice of black bread covered in butter, shave dark chocolate flakes, and pat down on the butter.

chocolate Sandwich

1 slice of black bread.
1 table spoon of butter
1 Block of dark chocolate

On a slice of black bread covered in butter shave dark chocolate flakes and pat down on the butter

BLINTZES

(Yiddish: blintse)

Survivors | **IRENE BUCHMAN AND OLGA JAEGER**

The Berkowicz sisters perfected their cooking and baking based on their collective memories of the taste, texture, and aroma of the foods their mother served. Their mother, Dobrish (Devorah), was known for her amazing baking, but it was done quickly and without the interference of children. For her, cooking and baking was a task that needed to get done along with caring for the children and working as a wigmaker. After the war, Irene and Olga were left only with memories, and through discussion with other survivor friends, sisters-in-law, and Good Housekeeping *recipes, they recreated their mother's food for their children to enjoy.*

Carol Buchman-Krutiansky (Irene's daughter) remembers: The blintzes were our family's favorite special treat for Shavuot. We knew that the Feast of Weeks was coming when my mother went out to get farmer cheese and pot cheese for the blintzes. A small delicacy store in Washington Heights sold the cheese, and my mother sent me to get it. I would lick my cheese-covered fingers, but my mother would yell at me that she needed it for her blintzes. When my mother became blind and was nearing the end of her life, she decided that her niece Debbie (Olga's daughter) would take over blintz making. To my mother, the blintzes had a very significant meaning. They reminded her of her childhood.

YIELDS ABOUT 30 BLINTZES

FOR THE CREPES:

2 cups all-purpose flour
¼ cup sugar
½ teaspoon fine salt
5 large eggs
2 cups milk
Vegetable oil or butter, as needed

Make the crepes: In a medium bowl, whisk the flour, sugar, and salt. In a large bowl using an electric mixer, beat the eggs and milk. Beat the flour mixture into the egg mixture until the batter is smooth.

Lightly coat a 6- to 8-inch nonstick skillet with oil or butter and heat over medium-high heat. Pour ¼ cup of the batter into the pan and quickly tilt the pan in a circular motion to cover the entire surface with a thin layer of batter. Cook the crepe until the center is set and dry and the edges and bottom are golden (do not let it turn brown), 1 to 1½ minutes, then use a spatula to remove it and turn it

FOR THE CHEESE FILLING:

Two 7½-ounce packages farmer cheese
1 large egg, beaten
½ cup sugar
1 teaspoon lemon zest
1 tablespoon lemon juice
1 teaspoon vanilla extract
¾ cup vegetable oil or butter

out onto a plate. Continue making crepes, stacking them on the plate separated by pieces of wax paper, until you have used all the batter. Let the crepes cool completely.

Make the filling: In a large bowl, combine the cheese, egg, sugar, lemon zest and juice, and vanilla. Using a fork, stir until incorporated.

To assemble and cook the blintzes, place a crepe on a work surface with the golden side facing down. Place 2 heaping tablespoons of the filling on the portion of the crepe closest to you, about an inch from the end. Fold the lower edge of the blintz up and over the filling, then fold the sides into the center, like you're folding an envelope. Roll from the bottom up and over the filling, tucking in the edges. Repeat with the remaining crepes and filling.

Heat ¾ cup oil or butter in a large nonstick skillet over medium heat. Working in batches, add the blintzes seam side down (make sure to leave a little space between them) and cook for about 2 minutes, until the bottom is browned and crisp. Turn the blintzes and cook for another 2 minutes, or until browned on the second side. Drain on paper towels and serve warm.

WAFFLES

Survivor | **ANNELIESE NOSSBAUM**

Anneliese's waffle recipe was tied to her will with a ribbon, as part of her legacy to her children. The recipe was handed down from their paternal grandmother. As Anneliese's children recall, their mother used the same waffle iron for decades. She made these waffles for any happy occasion: birthdays, holidays, anniversaries, homecomings, and "just because." They were a much-anticipated family favorite. More than once, Anneliese froze them and brought them to Israel, where her children lived for a few years, either herself or with the help of someone flying there. It was a taste of home. Anneliese would don an apron and spend hours prepping them and painstakingly baking—they were an expression of her love.

SERVES 8

3 eggs
1 cup (2 sticks) unsalted butter, melted and cooled
2 cups all-purpose flour
½ cup sugar, plus more for sprinkling
2 teaspoons baking powder
3 cups sour cream
A little milk, as needed, for consistency

Generously grease a waffle iron with nonstick cooking spray and leave to preheat.

In a large bowl, beat the eggs with the butter. In a separate bowl, whisk the flour, sugar, and baking powder. Mix the flour mixture into the egg mixture, then add the sour cream. Add some milk, a drop at a time, if needed to reach a somewhat thick, pourable consistency. Using a soup ladle or spouted measuring cup, pour a small amount of batter into the waffle iron to create a thin layer. Hold the lid open for a few seconds before closing. Let cook for about 2 to 3 minutes, or until golden on both sides (the cook time may need to be adjusted depending on the waffle iron—hers was old).

Remove the waffle from the iron and let cool slightly before sprinkling with sugar. Repeat with the remaining batter. Waffles can be frozen and defrosted at room temperature.

Note: These waffles are thin and crepe-like, not fluffy Belgian waffles.

CINNAMON BUNS

Survivor | **LOIS FLAMHOLZ**

When I was about 12 years old, I helped my mother with everything. I already knew then how to cook, how to bake. I learned how to do the challahs and braid them. I also learned how to make these cinnamon buns. I was the oldest of four children, and my mother wasn't a very healthy woman. She was permanently suffering from something. So I had to help with a lot of things. I grew up before my time.

YIELDS 12 BUNS

FOR THE DOUGH:

One ¼-ounce package active dry yeast
¾ cup warm water
2¼ cups all-purpose flour, plus more for the work surface
¼ cup granulated sugar
1 teaspoon salt
¼ cup vegetable shortening
1 egg
1 tablespoon unsalted butter, softened, plus more for greasing the pan

FOR THE CINNAMON-SUGAR TOPPING:

1½ teaspoons ground cinnamon
1½ teaspoons granulated sugar

FOR THE FROSTING:

¾ cup confectioners' sugar
Heavy cream or milk

Make the dough: In the bowl of an electric mixer, combine the yeast and water. In a separate bowl, whisk together 1 cup flour, sugar, and salt. Add the flour mixture to the dissolved yeast, then add the shortening and egg and beat 2 minutes at medium speed. Stir in the remaining 1¼ cups flour and blend well. Cover the bowl with a damp cloth and let the dough rise in a warm place (85°F) until doubled in size, about 1 hour.

Stir down the dough by beating 25 strokes. Turn the dough onto a well-floured, cloth-covered board. Roll into a rectangle, about 9 by 12 inches. Spread with the butter. Grease a 9-inch square pan.

Make the topping: Stir together the cinnamon and sugar. Sprinkle the cinnamon-sugar mixture evenly over the buttered surface of the dough. Beginning with a long side, tightly roll the dough into a log. Pinch the edge into the roll to seal it.

Cut the dough log into 12 equal pieces. Place the pieces cut side up in the prepared pan. Cover with the cloth and let rise in a warm place until doubled in size, about 40 minutes. Preheat the oven to 375°F.

Make the frosting: Whisk the confectioners' sugar with just enough cream or milk to be spreadable.

Bake the rolls for 25 minutes, or until golden brown. Turn the block of rolls onto a cutting board. Spread the frosting over the rolls while still hot. Let cool before pulling apart.

HUNGARIAN PANCAKES

(Hungarian: palacsinta)

Survivor | **EVA SZEPESI**

I remember an apricot tree in the garden by our house in Pesterzsébet, where I often played with my two cousins Zsuzsi and Vera, and my little brother Tamas. None of them came back from Auschwitz. I can still recall the scent of the ripe fruit. Until this day, my favorite pancakes are filled with apricot jam because of that vivid memory.

I remember that my mother and my grandma cooked the apricots in a big pot to make jam. Then they poured it into jars and put them in a prepared laundry basket made of willow sticks in which there was already a down pillow at the bottom. In the end, they covered the jars with a down pillow to draw in the warmth. That is how we had delicious jam all winter.

After baking, my mother would stack the pancakes one on top of the other and then spread the different fillings (poppy, nut, curd, jam), roll them together, and place them next to each other on the plate in the middle of the table. We children always ate the rolled pancakes with our hands, and the adults ate with forks.

After the war, we had pancakes almost every week. First, there was a soup, for example, a caraway soup, a sweet tomato soup, or a goulash soup, depending on what food was available, and then the pancakes as the main course. For my daughters Judith and Anita, there was first the sweet tomato soup and then the pancakes. Often, they stood next to me while I made the pancakes. They always impatiently waited for the pancakes to be done.

YIELDS 25 PANCAKES

3 eggs
2 egg yolks
¼ teaspoon salt
1 tablespoon sugar
2 cups all-purpose flour
2 cups milk
½ cup sparkling water (cold from the fridge), plus more if needed
Vegetable oil, for the pan
Apricot jam, cottage cheese, or chocolate spread, for filling

In a large bowl, whisk the eggs with the salt and sugar. Slowly add the flour and mix well. Add the milk and sparkling water to the dough and stir well. The batter should be a pourable consistency, like crepe batter, not too thick and not too thin. Stir in more sparkling water if it is too thick.

Brush a frying pan with oil and heat over medium-high. Pour enough batter into the pan to just cover the surface. Cook until golden, then flip and cook for another minute on the other side. Remove and repeat with the remainder of the batter.

Enjoy with various fillings, such as apricot jam, cottage cheese, or chocolate spread, and roll up the pancakes to serve.

LECHO

(Hungarian: lecsó)

Survivor | **DAVID MARKS**

My mother would make this dish for the family in the summer with fresh ingredients, and we all loved it. It was served as a summer side dish for lunch or dinner with fresh bread. Yum.

After I reunited with my sisters, we would teasingly compete over who makes it the best or the closest to our mother's. I must admit, when I visited sister Frimi in Chile, hers was memorable. Maybe the fresh ingredients in Chile made it taste better, or perhaps she added a secret ingredient. It was delicious, and I remember it still. I make an excellent one myself, though.

You must have patience when making this, and the flavors come out best if cooked very slowly. Of course, fresh ingredients are a key too. I grow my tomatoes and have chickens for fresh eggs. Not everyone has that luxury.

SERVES 1–3

1 tablespoon vegetable oil
1 medium onion, chopped
1 red bell pepper, chopped
1 large tomato, blanched, peeled, and chopped
2 cloves garlic, minced
Salt and black pepper
3 eggs

Heat the oil in a large skillet over medium heat. Add the onion and bell pepper and cook, stirring, until softened. Add the tomato, garlic, and salt and pepper to taste and cook another 10 to 15 minutes. Crack the eggs into the pan and cook until the egg whites are firm. Serve with vegetables and other side dishes.

Note: Traditionally the eggs are scrambled, but instead you can poach them in the sauce if you like, as shown in the photo here.

MAMALIGA

(Romanian: mămăligă)

Survivor | **ALEXANDER SPILBERG**

At home, my mother used to make mamaliga at least once a week. It's a typical Romanian side dish with many variations. My mother served it with plum jam, though she never taught us how to make it. She made it a little differently from how I learned to make it when I came to Canada. My kids love it, too, though they prefer to eat my mamaliga—they say my recipe is their favorite.

SERVES 2–4

3 cups cold water
1 teaspoon salt
½ cup cornmeal
9 ounces authentic Greek feta cheese
1 tablespoon butter, softened

Preheat the oven to 350°F. Pour the water into a medium pot and add the salt. Stir the cornmeal into the water. Turn the heat to medium and cook, stirring, until it comes to a boil. Reduce the heat and continue to cook, stirring continuously, for 5 to 8 minutes, until thickened.

Crumble the feta and spread half of it over a medium oven-safe platter or baking dish. Pour the cooked cornmeal carefully over the cheese and use a spatula or wooden spoon to smooth out the surface. Spread the butter onto the cornmeal, then top with the remaining feta. Bake for about 15 minutes, until the cornmeal is set and the cheese is melted.

To serve, place the hot platter on a trivet in the center of the table and use a large spoon to dish out onto small plates.

Note: We use spoons to eat this, often as a side dish for brunch.

SABBA SHLOMO'S MATZO BREI

Survivor | **RACHEL ROTH**

Rachel's son Ram remembers that Rachel described how they would wait for the last day of Passover (that was not Shabbat) to have this delicious treat as breakfast. During her childhood in Warsaw, they never had any leftover Matzoh after Passover! Rachel's husband, Shlomo, took over this family tradition and became famous among the children, grandchildren, and great-grandchildren for Sabba Shlomo's matzo brei, which he only made on Passover.

SERVES 4

4 sheets matzo (or more for a thicker matzo brei)
8 eggs, beaten
1 teaspoon salt, plus more if desired
½ teaspoon ground black pepper, plus more if desired
Vegetable oil, for the pan
Ground cinnamon, sugar, maple syrup, jam, or honey, for serving

Place the matzo in a large, deep bowl. Pour very hot water all over the matzo and allow to rest for about 30 seconds, until the matzo is soft. Squeeze out excess water and transfer to a dry bowl.

Using a large wooden spoon, mix in the eggs, salt, and pepper, breaking the matzo into approximately 1-inch chunks.

Heat the oil in a large skillet over medium heat. Add the matzo mixture and cook, stirring constantly as you would for scrambled eggs, until completely firm but still moist, about 5 minutes. Place in a bowl lined with paper towels to drain any excess oil.

Serve hot with any of the following sweet toppings: ground cinnamon, sugar, maple syrup, jam, or honey. Or season with additional salt and pepper for savory matzo brei.

BUNDT NOODLE KUGEL

Survivor | **RUTH WEBBER**

There are many different kugel variations. Savory or sweet, this baked casserole dish made from egg noodles or potatoes is a traditional Ashkenazi Jewish dish commonly served in northeastern Poland, Lithuania, and Galicia.

SERVES 12

½ cup butter, melted
¾ cup packed dark brown sugar
1 cup chopped walnuts (or other types of nuts or apples, if preferred)
4 eggs
⅔ cup granulated sugar
1 cup sour cream
¾ cup applesauce
1 teaspoon salt
½ teaspoon ground cinnamon
1 pound medium egg noodles, cooked and drained

Preheat the oven to 350°F and coat a Bundt pan with nonstick cooking spray.

Pour ¼ cup of the melted butter into the pan, tilting the pan to distribute it evenly. Sprinkle the brown sugar evenly over the butter. Top with the nuts.

In a large bowl, beat the eggs. Add the granulated sugar, sour cream, applesauce, remaining ¼ cup butter, salt, and cinnamon and whisk to combine. Add the noodles and thoroughly mix to coat. Pour into the prepared Bundt pan on top of the walnut mixture.

Bake for 1 hour, or until browned. Remove from the oven and let cool for 5 minutes. Run a knife around the edges or gently shake the kugel to loosen, then invert the pan onto a serving plate. Remove the pan; the nuts will be on top of the kugel.

SWEET NOODLE KUGEL

Survivor | **MICHAEL BORNSTEIN**
(submitted in memory of Sophie Bornstein, his mother)

Mike and his mom, Sophie, made several dairy meals each week that included borscht and potato, gefilte fish, lox or whitefish, cucumber salad with onions, and bagels. She always made kugel for Break Fast when all of his aunts, uncles, and cousins would congregate. Meals with the family were lively and full of song and laughter.

Mike has fond memories of his mom's kugel. The family tried many recipes until they came up with one that reminded Mike of his mom's. Sophie didn't have traditional written-down recipes, but the family hit upon this one after much trial and error. It's Mike's favorite. Mike's three daughters now enjoy making it for their families.

SERVES 8–10 AS A MAIN; 16–20 AS A SIDE OR DESSERT

1 pound wide egg noodles
1 cup cornflake crumbs
½ cup packed brown sugar
1 teaspoon ground cinnamon
½ cup (1 stick) butter
Two 8-ounce blocks cream cheese, softened
1 cup granulated sugar
8 eggs
2 cups milk

Preheat the oven to 350°F and grease a 9-by-13-inch baking dish.

Prepare the noodles according to package instructions, drain, and set aside to cool completely.

In a medium bowl, mix the cornflakes, brown sugar, and cinnamon. Set aside.

Using an electric mixer, cream together half of the butter, cream cheese, and granulated sugar in a large bowl. Beat in the eggs and milk and pour the mixture over the noodles. Toss to combine.

Pour the noodle mixture into the prepared baking dish and sprinkle with the cornflake topping. Dot with the remaining ¼ cup butter, then bake, uncovered, for 1 hour or until golden brown.

Note: This is a very easy recipe, filling and rich. It is a children's favorite and could be served as dessert.

NOODLE KUGEL

(Yiddish: lokshen kugel)

Survivor | **MIRIAM ZIEGLER**

What makes this dish particularly delicious is the combination of apples and pineapples. The pineapple seems like an unusual addition to kugel. Yet it gives the dish a fruity taste. That was my mother's invention: she gave me the recipe. And so that is how I continue to make it. You can make this recipe all year long, but I tend to cook it for holidays. I particularly like to make it for Rosh Hashana as it makes for a sweet new year. My family loves it and looks forward to it.

SERVES 20

Two 12-ounce packages medium egg noodles
1 teaspoon salt, for cooking the noodles
7 large eggs
2 cups sugar
2 tablespoons vegetable oil
20-ounce can crushed pineapple, partially drained (reserve half of the juice)
2 packets (about 2 tablespoons) vanilla sugar, or 2 teaspoons vanilla extract
3 medium apples, peeled, cored, and thinly sliced
½ cup raisins or dried cranberries (if desired)

Preheat the oven to 350°F. Lightly grease a 16-by-9½-inch glass baking dish (or two 8-by-5-inch dishes) with nonstick cooking spray.

Boil the noodles in salted water according to package directions until al dente. Drain and rinse under cold water. Set aside. In a large mixing bowl, whisk the eggs, then add the sugar, oil, pineapple, and vanilla sugar and mix well. Stir in the noodles. Add the apples and raisins, if desired, and mix well.

Pour the noodle mixture into the prepared baking dish and bake on the middle rack, uncovered, for 1 hour. You will know that the kugel is fully cooked when golden brown and the noodles on top appear crispy. Refrigerate, cut, and reheat to serve (it cuts best when cooled), or freeze and reheat as needed.

COMPOTE

Survivor | **BENJAMIN LESSER**

The story of this compote goes back to Munkatch, Hungary. My grandfather had a stately home on a major street called Sugar—an appropriate name for that sweet home. He had a big orchard and gardens (in the rose garden there was a sukkah made of wine bottles, and I remember seeing prisms of sunlight through the glass). Many kinds of berries and fruits grew in the orchard: raspberries, blueberries, apples, plums, and pears. The orchard also had a red lattice walkway with hanging grapes. Every year, we would line up there and somebody on the tree would drop pears to us. We'd make a big chain all the way to the house, maybe twenty kids. We put those pears in tissue paper in the attic to ripen. And of course, we made compote.

When I was a child, we would always pick the fruit while it was hard, not yet ripe. Then we would put all of it in the attic to ripen. Once ripe, pears and all the other fruit picked from my grandfather's orchard would be sliced and then cooked in the water.

When I make this recipe, I pick fresh pears from my trees, or if I need more fruit, I buy it dried, especially prunes, and place them in the water to achieve the same result.

SERVES 4–6

3 cups pitted dried prunes
3 cups dried apricots
2 cups dried peaches
1 cup dried pears
1 cup dried apple rings
1 cup raisins or cranberries
1 or 2 lemon slices
½ cup packed light brown sugar
½ cup orange juice
2 tablespoons maple syrup
½ cup sweet wine, or to taste
¼ teaspoon ground cinnamon
Pinch of cloves

Combine the dried fruit and lemon slices in a 6-quart pot and place over medium heat. Add the brown sugar, orange juice, maple syrup, wine, and spices and bring to a boil. Cover, reduce the heat, and simmer for 15 minutes. Set aside to cool; the fruit will swell as it cools. Store in airtight containers and refrigerate, or enjoy warm (*fantastic over ice cream!*).

Note: I use only unsweetened dried fruit without sulfates. I like to freeze portions in 6-ounce containers or plastic baggies so that they don't take up much room in the freezer. Then they can be used whenever you desire a taste of the old country, and they help to keep your system flowing smoothly after heavy meals.

NOSHES *and* SIDES

תוספות ונשנושים

HUNGARIAN LAYERED POTATOES WITH CHEESE

(Hungarian: rakott krumpli)

Survivor | **DAVID MARKS**

Rakott krumpli is a Hungarian layered casserole, traditionally made with potatoes, sour cream, hard-boiled eggs, and bread crumbs. Before the war, this was a special meal since chicken eggs were rationed and not always available. It was always a memorable meal to share with a family: usually served after a soup as the main meal. The memory of this meal takes me back to when I was a little boy when we had free-range chickens that wandered the property in the day and returned to their coop at night. Each morning, we children had to take turns sticking our fingers inside each chicken to feel for an egg. If we felt an egg, we kept that chicken in the coop rather than letting it roam, risking that it would lay the egg in the yard somewhere. My younger sister, Frimi, could not bear to do it and would pay me to take her turn. I would use the money to buy screws and nails for woodworking. When the war started, we had to give most of our eggs to the military, and our family eggs were rationed and very limited for the size of our family. Now, in my house in Connecticut, I raise chickens, enjoy their eggs, and share them with neighbors.

SERVES 10

6 medium potatoes (about 3 pounds)
10 large eggs
Butter or margarine, for greasing the pan
5 cups sour cream
1 cup cottage cheese
1 teaspoon salt
1 teaspoon paprika
½ cup seasoned bread crumbs

Peel potatoes and place in a large pot with water. Nestle 9 of the eggs around the perimeter of the pot. Put the pot over medium heat and bring to a boil. Once the water comes to a boil, reduce the heat to medium-low. Set a timer for 10 minutes for the eggs. When done, remove the eggs using a slotted spoon and let cool. Continue to cook the potatoes until they are tender. Drain the potatoes and set aside to cool.

Preheat the oven to 350°F. Grease a 9-by-13-inch baking pan with butter or margarine.

When the potatoes are cool enough to handle, slice them into flat disks. Peel and slice the eggs, being careful to retain a bit of the yolk and white in each slice. In a large bowl, mix 4 cups of the sour cream with the cottage cheese, salt, and paprika.

Place a layer of potato slices on the bottom of the baking pan. Dollop about half of the dairy mixture evenly over the potatoes. Add a layer of sliced eggs, using about half of the eggs. Sprinkle evenly with about a third of the bread crumbs. Repeat the layering process, using up all the potatoes, dairy mixture, and eggs. Sprinkle with about half of the remaining bread crumbs.

For the topping, whisk together the remaining 1 cup sour cream and the raw egg. Spread this mixture over the top of the pan. Sprinkle the remaining bread crumbs over the top. Bake until golden brown and bubbling.

Note: An essential ingredient that makes this dish unique is the toasted bread crumbs that add color and crunch. I use Yukon Gold potatoes, fresh chicken eggs, sour cream, and cottage cheese. Some recipes call for added shredded mild cheese, onions, or sausage, but we always ate it without.

HUNGARIAN LAYERED POTATOES

(Hungarian: rakott krumpli)

Survivor | **EVA SHAINBLUM**

I was sixteen years old when in 1944, one day after Shavuot, my entire family was deported to Auschwitz-Birkenau. The last meal we had on the night before the deportation to Auschwitz was this particular dish of rakott-krumpli. I don't know how we were able to get the ingredients. I will never forget this, as it was our last meal together as a family.

Before the war, my mother worked, so I learned most dishes from one of her friends who got laid off. In Hungary, we didn't have meat every day, so we ate a lot of dairy dishes. This recipe was one of our favorites—mine and my daughter's. While it's a very primitive recipe, it's delicious. It's great comfort food.

SERVES 10 AS A SIDE DISH; 4–6 AS A MAIN DISH

4 tablespoons butter or margarine
6 medium potatoes
5 hard-boiled eggs, peeled
2 cups sour cream
1½ cups bread crumbs
Salt and black pepper

Preheat the oven to 350°F and grease a casserole dish with butter or margarine.

Boil the whole potatoes until tender but still firm. Set aside to cool.

Slice the cooled potatoes and the hard-boiled eggs into ¼-inch rounds and sprinkle them with salt and pepper to taste. Set aside some of the sour cream and bread crumbs for the topping.

In the prepared casserole dish, make a layer of potatoes, followed by layers of eggs, bread crumbs, and sour cream. Repeat layers until the dish is full; top with the reserved sour cream and bread crumbs. Bake for 40 minutes or until brown on top.

Note: You can use any potatoes you want for this recipe. Boil the potatoes with the skin on and then peel after they cool down.

EGGPLANT APPETIZER DIP

Survivor | **DAVID MARKS**

In my household, we make this dip seasonally. It's a simple side dish that can be served with bread. I like to offer it as an appetizer with crackers and a cocktail.

SERVES 8–12

2 large eggplants
1 yellow onion, chopped
2 cloves garlic, peeled
½ teaspoon salt
½ teaspoon ground black pepper
½ cup mayonnaise
Sprinkle of paprika
Crackers or bread rounds

Preheat the oven to 350°F.

Place the eggplants on a baking sheet and bake until the skin splits and the flesh softens, 30 to 45 minutes. Let cool slightly, then peel off the skin, slice open each eggplant, and place the crushed flesh into a sieve to drain.

Combine the drained eggplant flesh, the onion, garlic, salt, pepper, and mayonnaise in a blender and blend until creamy. Transfer to a bowl, sprinkle with paprika, and serve with crackers or bread rounds for dipping.

HUMMUS

Survivors | **IRENE BUCHMAN AND OLGA JAEGER**

SERVES 4

15-ounce can chickpeas, drained and rinsed
1 clove garlic, peeled
3 tablespoons tahini
Juice of ½ lemon (about 2 tablespoons)
6 tablespoons water
1 teaspoon ground cumin
½ teaspoon salt

Put all the ingredients into a food processor. Blend until smooth, scraping down the sides a couple of times. Add more water if too thick, a tablespoon at a time to reach desired consistency. Add more of the seasonings to suit your palate, if you like. Blend again and serve.

EGGPLANT SALAD

Survivor | **ELISABETH CITROM**

Whenever I visited New York, there were two specialties that my children always wanted: my vegetable soup and this eggplant salad. It's a lovely dish. I like to serve it with good rye bread. I also prefer to make this by hand because using a food processor would make the consistency too smooth.

SERVES 6–8

- 3 large eggplants
- 1 medium to large yellow onion, finely chopped
- 2 tablespoons distilled white vinegar
- ½–1 teaspoon salt, or to taste
- Pinch of sugar (optional; takes the edge off the vinegar)
- ½ cup vegetable oil

Hold the eggplants directly over a stove-top burner over high heat and cook, turning with tongs to get at all sides, until the skin is charred and the eggplants are very soft, about 30 minutes. Set aside to cool on a platter.

When the eggplants are cool enough to touch, remove the blackened skin. Place them in a colander and rinse quickly with cold water to remove some of the remaining burnt skin.

Place the flesh in a large bowl. Add the onion, vinegar, salt, and sugar, if using. Slowly add the oil while mixing with a wooden spoon, making sure to make the salad smooth.

MATBUCHA

Survivors | **IRENE BUCHMAN AND OLGA JAEGER**

With roots in North African cuisine, matbucha is a robustly flavorful side dish that can be eaten as a dip with bread or raw vegetables or, if you like, as a relish alongside roast meats. It is also delicious as a topping for crostini spread with a soft cheese.

SERVES 2-3

5 large roma tomatoes, roughly chopped
5 cloves garlic, peeled
½ red bell pepper, roughly chopped
½ jalapeño, roughly chopped
1 teaspoon paprika
3 tablespoons olive oil
½ teaspoon sugar, plus more to taste
½ teaspoon salt, plus more to taste

In a food processor, combine the tomatoes, garlic, red pepper, and jalapeño and pulse until broken down into a chunky mixture. Transfer to a large saucepan and bring to a simmer over medium heat. Reduce the heat to low and cook for about 1 hour 45 minutes. Add the paprika and olive oil along with the sugar and salt and cook for an additional 15 minutes. Serve.

ISRAELI SALAD

Survivor | **EVA SZEPESI**

I love this fresh and joyful Israeli salad. I incorporated this recipe into my cooking repertoire after my two youngest grandchildren went to Israel following high school and worked in a kibbutz and volunteer service with autistic people. They brought this refreshing and healthy salad recipe with them.

And now when my two older grandchildren visit from Belgium with my three great-grandchildren, there is always this colorful salad on the breakfast table.

SERVES 4

Several Persian cucumbers, sliced, or 1 regular cucumber, finely diced
4 tomatoes, seeded and diced, or 20 grape tomatoes, halved
1 red bell pepper, diced or cut into strips
Juice of 2 lemons, or more to taste
2 tablespoons olive oil
½ tablespoon salt, or more to taste
1 avocado, pitted, peeled, and diced (optional)
Leaves from a few sprigs of fresh mint

Combine the cucumber, tomatoes, and red pepper in a medium salad bowl. Add the lemon juice, oil, and salt and stir gently. Taste it, and maybe you need more of the salt or the lemon juice.

If you like, you can also add diced avocado. What you get is a fresh, light, and colorful salad. Stir in the mint and serve.

CHOPPED LIVER

(Yiddish: gehakte leber)

Survivor | **ROSALIE SIMON**

The recipe presented here has not changed over time. This dish evokes memories of sharing meals with a family. We serve it as an appetizer. Depending on the day of the week, chopped liver can be followed by a Saturday cholent or a Shabbat dinner matzo ball soup, chicken, potato kugel, and tzimmes.

SERVES 10–12

1 pound calf's liver
2–3 large yellow onions, chopped
3 tablespoons vegetable oil
3 hard-boiled eggs, peeled and roughly chopped
Salt and black pepper

Broil liver until done (do not dry out). Sauté onions with oil until golden brown. Grind all ingredients together in a meat grinder or food processor. For a finer consistency, grind twice and stir together with a spoon. Serve with crackers or vegetables for dipping.

Note: It takes 5 to 10 minutes for the liver to be done in the broiler. Make sure it is not red inside.

Chopped liver

1 pound of calves liver
2-3 large onions chopped depends on size
3 hard boiled eggs
salt & pepper to taste

broil liver until done do not dry out
saute onions until golden brown with oil
grind everything together
liver, eggs, onions salt & pepper
for a finer consistency grind twice,
mix it all up with a spoon

CUCUMBER SALAD

Survivor | **MIRIAM ZIEGLER**

This vinegary cucumber salad has always been our favorite special Shabbat and holidays side dish. I also like to make it when I have special guests over. The tangy taste of the salad goes very well with meat, especially roast beef, chicken cutlets, or veal. It tastes best when served chilled. Children love it too!

The recipe goes back to my grandmother, who passed it on to my mother, who then passed it on to me. I, in return, have shared it with my daughters and granddaughters. Five generations have loved and made it! The recipe has not changed at all over the years. I always say that if it's not broken, don't fix it.

SERVES 8

2 large English cucumbers
1 tablespoon salt
½–1 cup cold water
¼ cup distilled white vinegar
3 teaspoons sugar
1–2 teaspoons chopped fresh dill (optional)
Sweet paprika, for garnish

Peel the cucumbers, if you like, then carefully slice them crosswise using a mandoline set with a 3-millimeter blade. (You can use a chef's knife, but the mandoline is quicker and makes more even slices.)

Put the cucumbers in a large bowl and add the salt. Toss to coat, then set aside for 1 hour to sweat out the moisture. Drain thoroughly in a colander, using your hands to press out as much water as possible. Transfer the cucumbers to a large plastic or glass container with a lid.

In a small bowl, stir the water and vinegar with the sugar until it dissolves. If desired, add fresh dill. Pour the liquid over the cucumbers and toss to coat. Cover and chill in the refrigerator for at least 2 hours. Serve cold, sprinkled with sweet paprika.

Note: The salad keeps well in the refrigerator. It can last a few days.

GREEN BEANS IN DILL SAUCE

Survivor | **VLAD MUNK**

Vlad likes to serve this dish with boiled beef or hard-boiled eggs and boiled potatoes.

SERVES 4–6

1 pound green beans, fresh, frozen, or canned
Salt
4 tablespoons butter
4 tablespoons all-purpose flour
4 cups milk
1 bunch fresh dill, chopped
1 tablespoon sugar (or sugar substitute)
2–3 tablespoons distilled white vinegar
3/4 cup whipping cream

If using fresh or frozen green beans, cook them first in salted boiling water until tender, 3 to 5 minutes.

In a large frying pan or sauté pan, heat the butter over medium heat until melted and foamy. Add the flour and stir constantly until a smooth, light yellow roux forms. Add the milk and continue to stir until it comes to a boil. Add the dill, season with salt, reduce the heat to low, and cook, stirring occasionally, until thickened, 20 to 25 minutes.

Add the sugar, vinegar to taste, and whipping cream and heat until the sugar is dissolved. Fold the beans into the sauce, or serve the sauce on top of the warm beans.

TRADITIONAL RED CABBAGE

(German: Rotkohl)

Survivor | **CLAIRE HEYMANN**

Eating this food connects me to my family. Back in Germany, this red cabbage dish was a family favorite. It is a seasonal, cold-weather side dish that goes very well with roast beef and brisket. What makes this dish particularly delicious is the combination of the savory flavor with the right touch of sweetness.

SERVES 10

- 1 medium yellow onion, halved and sliced
- 1 medium apple (McIntosh or Granny Smith), cored and grated
- 1 medium red cabbage, cored and shredded (about 8 cups)
- ⅓ cup sugar
- ⅓ cup distilled white vinegar
- ¾ teaspoon salt
- ¼ teaspoon ground black pepper
- ½ teaspoon ground cloves, or 4 whole cloves (optional)

Coat a medium Dutch oven with nonstick cooking spray and heat over medium heat. Add the onion and apple and cook until the onion is tender, about 5 minutes. Stir in the cabbage, sugar, vinegar, salt, pepper, and cloves, if desired, and cook, stirring occasionally, until the cabbage is very soft, about 1 hour. Serve warm or cold.

Note: If you don't have a Dutch oven, any good-quality pot will do.

CREAMED SPINACH

Survivor | **EVA KERENYI**

Eva never knew how to cook before the war. She learned from cookbooks after she was married in Toronto.

Her son John recalls: When we were looking for these recipes, we found a file folder with many papers and stuff clipped from magazines and newspapers or handwritten recipes she got from her friends. We looked through all of that. We found some great stuff, but we didn't see the spinach or the strawberry soup recipes that were in her head. She never wrote them down. But I remember that when I was a kid, my mother would be on the phone with people saying, "Oh, this is really easy. Write this down." And that's how she shared it with everyone.

My mother used to prepare this spinach dish every time her mother would visit us. It's connected to this memory of three generations reconnecting and sharing meals. The story of this dish becoming a staple in our family goes back to my mom wanting us to eat healthily. As we didn't like steamed or boiled spinach, she came up with a savory, creamy, tasty dish we all loved.

I have always loved how my mom personalized this recipe by adding whipped cream to it. I think it was my mom's secret ingredient that made all the difference. My mother taught me how to make some old family dishes during the pandemic: her lecho (Hungarian vegetable stew) and rakott krumpli (a potato and cheese dish).

SERVES 6

1 tablespoon salt
24 ounces fresh baby spinach
1 large bread roll
Milk
2 tablespoons butter
2 tablespoons all-purpose flour
2 cloves garlic, minced
1½ cups heavy cream
2 eggs, beaten

Bring 2 quarts of water and the salt to a boil in a large pot. Add the spinach. Cook until wilted, strain, and let cool.

Cut the roll in half and soak it in milk. Squeeze the bread to remove excess.

In a large saucepan over medium-low heat, melt the butter and stir in the flour. Add the garlic, cream, and 2 tablespoons of milk and cook, continuing to stir, until the sauce thickens. Stir in the drained spinach and the bread. Add the eggs in a slow and steady stream, stirring constantly. Continue to cook for about 2 minutes, until the creamed spinach thickens further. Serve hot.

DAVID'S SPINACH

(Hungarian: spenòt)

Survivor | **DAVID MARKS**

What makes this dish particularly delicious are the garlic and fresh eggs. It could be a side for many meals, but I pair it with beef.

SERVES 4

One 12-ounce package fresh spinach
Salt
2 teaspoons vegetable oil
1 small sweet onion, chopped
2 cloves garlic, peeled
2 or 3 eggs, beaten

Drop the spinach into a pot of salted boiling water and stir to wilt all the leaves. Immediately remove the blanched spinach to a bowl of ice water to stop the cooking process.

Drain and put the spinach into a blender with the oil, onion, garlic, and eggs; blend just until smooth. (Do not over-blend.)

Cook on top of the stove over medium heat, stirring constantly, until set. Salt to your liking once served.

RICE IN THE OVEN

Survivor | **MIRIAM ZIEGLER**

This rice-in-the-oven recipe is both my daughter Debbie's and my grandson Jacob's favorite dish. I usually pair it with Friday night roasted chicken. What makes it remarkably delicious is the combination of the flavors of the onion soup, the mushrooms, and the soy sauce.

I am not picky when it comes to the preferred type of mushroom I like to use. We use both sliced and whole canned mushrooms.

SERVES 12

2 cups long-grain white rice
4 cups cold water
½–1 cup vegetable oil
4-ounce can whole mushrooms, drained
4-ounce can sliced mushrooms
2-ounce package kosher onion soup mix
1 tablespoon low-sodium soy sauce

Preheat the oven to 350°F and coat the bottom and sides of a 2½- to 3-quart covered casserole dish with nonstick cooking spray.

Place all the ingredients into the casserole and stir with a spoon to combine. Cover and bake for 1 hour 15 minutes. You will know that the rice is ready when all the liquid appears to have disappeared. Stir and serve as a side dish.

BOILED POTATO

Survivor | **EUGENE GINTER**

We came to the United States in April 1950. I remember that in the summertime, we had no air-conditioning, only a fan. What can you digest when it gets so hot? Very little. So my mother would make boiled potatoes. You put them on a plate and mash them up, put buttermilk over it, and that would be dinner. It was 90 degrees outside with 90 percent humidity; we were sweating. We really couldn't eat chicken and this or that—we had buttermilk and potato.

My mother would only use Idaho or russet potatoes. She would not add any salt or condiments.

SERVES 1 OR MORE

Potatoes (1 per person)
Buttermilk (1/4 to 1/2 cup per person)

Boil potatoes. Mash. Cover the mashed potato with buttermilk.

HUNGARIAN POTATOES

Survivor | **ALEXANDER SPILBERG**

I have a clear memory of my mother making these Hungarian potatoes for us when I was a kid. It is a hearty side dish that pairs well with a brisket of beef, steak, or chicken. If you keep the skins on potatoes instead of peeling them before boiling, you add extra flavor to the dish.

SERVES 2

2 large potatoes, preferably russet
1 large yellow onion, diced
3 tablespoons vegetable oil
½ teaspoon Hungarian paprika
Salt

Wash and boil the potatoes, skins on, until tender.

While the potatoes cook, fry the diced onion in a generous amount of oil. Add paprika and salt and cook until golden.

When the potatoes are cooked through, drain and peel them, then chop into small pieces and add to the onions. Add more salt to taste and toss well. Continue frying for approximately 5 minutes, stirring occasionally. Serve with a meal.

POTATO KUGEL

Survivor | **LEA ROTH**

This savory kugel was among the foods that we made for Shabbat. Potatoes were a staple in our house. We grew them in our yard amongst many other vegetables that we ate in various ways daily. For Shabbat, we prepared this potato kugel and baked it with our cholent in a communal oven overnight. A big brick oven was heated all day Friday and turned off before Shabbat. It stayed warm well into midday Saturday. Several families used this oven, and each would have their name inscribed on their utensils. Every family would come to Shabbat to pick up their pots of food.

SERVES 12

5 medium potatoes
4 eggs
1¼ cups schmaltz (goose or chicken fat) or vegetable oil
Salt and black pepper

Preheat the oven to 200°F.

Peel and grate the potatoes by hand or using the shredding blade on a food processor (some people say that hand-grated potatoes taste better!). Leave the potatoes to drain slightly in a colander for a few minutes. In a large bowl, combine the grated potatoes, eggs, and schmaltz. Season with salt and pepper, then pour the potato mixture into a deep casserole dish or baking pan. Bake overnight, for 10 to 12 hours. You will know that the kugel is fully cooked when the crust becomes a darker shade of brown.

Note: You can use any potatoes for this recipe, but the red ones are the ones I recommend.

SOUPS *and* DUMPLINGS

מרקים וכופתאות

MATZO BALL SOUP

Survivor | **EVA SZEPESI**

After the Shoah, I had no mother who could teach me how to cook and bake, so I learned as much as I could from my husband Andor's mother, Ilonka Schwarcz. I learned this recipe from my mother-in-law when I was seventeen. I remember how she would light the Shabbat candles behind closed curtains in Budapest and then serve this soul-warming soup on Passover or Shabbat. Today my daughters Judith and Anita also cook this matzo ball soup for their families according to Ilonka's recipe.

SERVES 10

FOR THE CHICKEN SOUP:

1 soup chicken
3 quarts chicken broth
3 large carrots
1 onion, whole, skin on
1 kohlrabi, diced
1 parsnip, diced
1 celery bulb
3 cloves garlic
10 whole black peppercorns
Salt, to taste
Pinch of saffron or paprika

FOR THE MATZO BALLS:

5 pieces matzo
5 eggs
2 tablespoons chicken fat
½ teaspoon salt
½ teaspoon black pepper
½ teaspoon ground nutmeg
½ cup matzo flour
Fresh dill or flat-leaf parsley, for garnish

Make the soup: Put the chicken in a big stockpot and cover it with water. Bring to a boil over high heat and boil for 15 minutes. Remove the white foam that floats to the top and reduce the heat to medium. Remove the white foam that rises a second time and then add all the other soup ingredients to the pot. Reduce the heat to low, partially cover, and simmer for 1 hour, or until the chicken is cooked. Remove the breast and reserve it to return it to the soup later. Continue to cook the soup for 2 more hours, skimming off any white foam.

Make the matzo balls: Soak the matzo in warm water for about 10 minutes. In a large bowl, beat the eggs with a fork. Add the chicken fat, salt, pepper, and nutmeg and stir. Remove the soaked matzo from the water, slide it into the eggs, and mix well. Stir in the matzo flour. Cover and refrigerate for about 20 minutes, then scoop 2-tablespoon portions of dough and form balls with wet hands. Add the balls to the boiling soup or a pot of salted boiling water, lower the heat to maintain a simmer, cover, and cook for about 20 minutes, until the matzo balls are cooked through and starting to sink.

To serve, remove the carrots, onion, and chicken from the soup and strain the soup through a sieve. Serve the clear soup with a piece of carrot, some chicken, a matzo ball, and some dill or parsley.

RACHEL'S FANTASTICAL CHICKEN SOUP

Survivor | **RACHEL ROTH**

After the war, Rachel Roth described a torturous roll call in the camp when prisoners were forced to stand outside in the freezing winter night. She distracted herself and her fellow prisoners by slowly describing Friday Shabbat dinner preparations at her home in prewar Warsaw. One of the recipes she would tell her fellow prisoners about was this soup—what her family at home now calls Rachel's Fantastical Chicken Soup. It isn't Shabbat without it.

SERVES 4

4-pound chicken
1 clove garlic, peeled
3 sprigs fresh parsley
3 sprigs fresh dill
1 tablespoon coarsely ground black pepper, or to taste
1 tablespoon salt, or to taste
2 large onions, quartered
5 carrots, peeled and halved
3 stalks celery, sliced into ½-inch pieces
8 ounces thin egg noodles
¼ small savoy cabbage

Put the chicken in a large stockpot. Cover with water and bring to a boil over high heat. Add the garlic, parsley, dill, pepper, and salt, then cover, reduce the heat to low, and simmer for 2 to 2½ hours, adding the onions, carrots, and celery for the last hour of the cooking time.

Remove and bone the chicken, pulling the meat into large chunks. Add the noodles and cabbage to the pot and cook for 5 minutes, or until the noodles and cabbage are softened. Return the chicken to the broth to heat through before serving.

CHICKEN SOUP

Survivor | **EUGENE GINTER**

I have vivid memories of keeping my mother company while she cooked this soup for me. She would put the minute steak in the soup to give it more body. She would usually make it for the family on Fridays. Sitting together to enjoy a bowl full of this nourishing soup underscored the fact that all three of us survived. We were all together again.

SERVES 4–6

1 whole chicken, cut into quarters (include the heart and stomach)
2 pieces (about 1 pound) minute steak or flanken
1 package soup greens
Fresh dill

Combine all ingredients. Cook until the meat comes off the bone, about 1 hour or more.

Note: My mother always added the soup greens that consisted of turnips, celery, parsley, dill, carrots, and onions. If you use flanken, then just one box of soup greens is necessary.

Chicken Soup.

One whole chicken cut into quarters
(include heart & stomach)

2 Pieces minute steak or flanken
approximately one pound.

1 package soup greens
Some fresh dill

Combine all ingredients
Cook until the meat comes off the bone,
about One hour or more.

DUMPLINGS

(Yiddish: kreplach)

Survivors | **IRENE BUCHMAN AND OLGA JAEGER**

These small dumplings, made from flour, water, and eggs, come with a variety of fillings and are traditionally served in chicken soup. Irene's daughter Carol remembers that in their family, the kreplach was a delicacy, but the dough was very time-consuming and took a lot of work. Irene and Olga did not make it often. Olga spent a lot of time with her daughter Debbie teaching her the recipe. According to Debbie, Olga and Irene recreated the original kreplach recipe based on the memory of their mother making it before the war. The recipe was lost during the war, but they worked hard to recreate it. What we have today is as close to the original as they could get.

Irene and Olga's recipes were perfected over the years: Irene, the incredible baker and Olga, the master chef. Both understood the fine art of taste, texture, and presentation. The sisters brought out the best in each other. It was a contest between the two sisters to see who created the dish that came closest to "the Mama's." The two sisters were often found debating the exact ingredients and quantities used in the dish. Carol recalls that it was comical to listen and learn the "art of food dissection." As their children and grandchildren will attest, they are the "best cookers"—and master chefs could learn a thing or two from Irene and Olga.

Note: Recipe on page 64.

SERVES 10–12

FOR THE FILLING (USE RESERVED INGREDIENTS FROM PREPARED CHICKEN SOUP):

2 cups roughly chopped chicken
1 onion, from the soup
1 carrot, from the soup
1 stalk celery, from the soup
1 extra-large egg, beaten
Salt, to taste
Ground black pepper, to taste
Finely minced fresh herbs, such as chives, parsley, or dill (optional)

FOR THE DOUGH:

3 extra-large eggs
1 teaspoon kosher salt
2 cups all-purpose flour, plus more as needed

Note: For the filling, use reserved ingredients from the prepared chicken soup.

Prepare chicken soup based on your favorite recipe. It should include the ingredients you will need for the kreplach filling: chicken, onion, carrot, and celery.

Once the chicken becomes tender, remove all the chicken to a large shallow bowl to let it cool. Remove onion pieces, carrot pieces, and celery pieces from the pot and set them aside to use in the filling. Reserve the broth for serving later with the kreplach. Discard any remaining vegetables.

Prepare the filling: Once the chicken is cool enough to handle, transfer it to a cutting board. Using your hands or a fork and knife, remove and discard the skin and bones. Roughly chop up the meat and reserve 2 cups to be used for the kreplach. Save the remaining meat for another purpose, such as chicken salad.

Place the chopped chicken and the reserved vegetable pieces in a food processor. Using the S-shaped blade, chop until the mixture resembles coarse bread crumbs. (Alternatively, you may finely mince the chicken and vegetables with a large chef's knife on a cutting board.) Stir in the egg and salt and pepper and mix to combine. Set aside.

Prepare the dough: With a fork, beat together the eggs and salt in a large bowl. Mix in the flour until the dough comes together in a soft ball.

On a clean, floured surface, roll out the dough until it is very thin. You may need to do this in two batches, depending upon your workspace. Cut out disks that are 3 inches in diameter. Place a scant teaspoon of filling in the center of each disk of dough, pressing the edges firmly to seal.

Carefully drop the kreplach into a large pot of salted boiling water. Cook for about 10 minutes, then add to chicken soup.

Top with the fresh herbs if you like.

RUTH'S CHICKEN SOUP

Survivor | **RUTH WEBBER**

Before the war, this soup was always a staple in our home—I remember it being served at my maternal grandparents' house for every Shabbat.

My family and I prefer to cook a clear chicken soup, so we discard the chicken and vegetables at the end. Also, it's important to note that I never let the soup boil—it should always be on a slow simmer. When the soup is reheated, I add dill for extra flavor (and take it out before serving).

SERVES 12

5-pound chicken, plus additional turkey leg, wing, or neck, or extra chicken parts (not gizzards), skin and extra fat removed
14 cups water
1 large onion, whole, with skin on (to give the soup more color)
3 leeks, white part only, halved
4 carrots
3 ribs celery
2 parsnips
Rutabagas, turnips, or kohlrabi, cubed (optional, if available)
2 bay leaves
4–5 stalks fresh dill
1 cup loosely packed fresh flat-leaf parsley with the stems
Salt
Ground white pepper or 10 whole black peppercorns

In a large stockpot, combine the chicken, extra poultry, and water and slowly bring to a boil. When the soup comes to a boil, a foam will form on the top. As it cooks, skim the foam continuously until most of it is removed.

Add the onion, leeks, carrots, celery, parsnips, rutabagas, and bay leaves. Bring to a simmer, then reduce the heat to low.

Cover and cook the soup slowly, until the chicken is soft, about 2 to 2½ hours. I don't actually pay attention to how long. Two hours, it might be more. Keep skimming the soup as needed to get rid of the foam. About 10 minutes before the soup is finished cooking, add dill and parsley Season to taste with salt and pepper.

Cook for the last 10 to 15 minutes, then remove the vegetables and the chicken and extra poultry. Pour the soup through a sieve and refrigerate until the fat rises to the top. If you like, skim off the fat for fat-free soup, then reheat and serve.

Notes: This soup recipe calls for a pullet, a mature chicken often available at kosher butcher shops near the High Holy Days. If unavailable, one can use other kinds of chicken and poultry pieces. I save the wings and bones from chickens I've cooked previously—or a bone from a turkey—and put those into the pot as well. And the more vegetables you use, the more flavor the soup will have (I like to use kohlrabi or whatever winter vegetables are available).

VEGETABLE SOUP WITH DUMPLINGS

Survivor | **ELISABETH CITROM**

This is a delicious everyday recipe. It's my son Joel's favorite vegetable soup. All of my grandchildren love it too. When I would visit them in New York, this was one of the specialties they always wanted. I wish I could make it for them now. If it were not for the pandemic, I would make it for the whole family.

SERVES 6–8

FOR THE SOUP:

4 tablespoons vegetable oil
1 large yellow onion, finely chopped
2 stalks celery, diced
Salt and black pepper
3 vegetable bouillon cubes
½ red bell pepper
5 large carrots, cut into matchsticks
2 large potatoes, cubed
2 parsnips, cut into matchsticks
1 cup frozen green peas

FOR THE DUMPLINGS:

2 eggs
1 teaspoon vegetable oil
1 teaspoon salt
½ cup all-purpose flour, or more if needed

Make the soup: In a large pot, heat the vegetable oil over medium heat. Add the onion and celery and sauté until tender, about 5 minutes. Add 4 cups of water and bring to a boil, then add salt and pepper to taste, followed by the bouillon, red pepper, carrots, potatoes, and parsnips. (Liquid should cover the vegetables by a few inches; add more water and seasonings as needed.) Reduce the heat and simmer until the potatoes are just cooked through, about 30 minutes.

Make the dumplings: While the soup simmers, in a medium bowl, beat the eggs with the oil. Whisk in the salt, then gradually beat in the flour, adding more if needed to make a soft dough. Use a tablespoon to shape the dough into small dumplings, then slowly drop them into the simmering soup. Wait a few seconds between additions. Simmer for another 10 minutes, or until the dumplings are cooked through.

Gently stir in the peas. Discard the red pepper and ladle the soup and dumplings into serving bowls.

LIVER DUMPLINGS IN BEEF BROTH

Survivor | **VLAD MUNK**

I have a recipe for the Sunday lunch, which I have always loved. It's connected to a particular memory I have of my mom in our prewar kitchen. My mother often made roast beef for Sunday dinner. I loved to have beef soup for Sunday lunch, made from marrow bones and root vegetables that you cook until everything is soft. My mom would call me into the kitchen, and she would take out the bone and spread the marrow on toast. I loved this.

SERVES 3–4

6 cups beef broth
2 tablespoons butter (or margarine, not oil), softened
1 egg
4 ounces calf's liver, cleaned and ground (see note)
½ clove garlic, crushed, or a pinch of marjoram
Dash of salt
Dash of ground black pepper
1–1½ cups bread crumbs, or more as needed

In a large pot, bring the beef broth to a simmer over medium heat.

In a large bowl, cream the butter and egg together. Add the liver, garlic, salt, and pepper and mix to combine. Mix in enough of the bread crumbs to create a stiff dough.

Using wet hands, form the dough into small balls, about the size of a walnut. Test the dough by boiling just 1 dumpling in the beef broth to make sure it does not fall apart. If the dough is not thick enough to adhere, add more bread crumbs and test another ball. When the consistency is right, simmer the dumplings in the broth for 3 to 5 minutes, until cooked through.

Note: Ask your butcher to grind the liver, or dice the liver yourself then place it in a food processor and pulse until smooth.

PLUM DUMPLINGS

(Hungarian: szilvás gombóc)

Survivor | **EVA SZEPESI**

Eva's grandson Leroy Schwarz recalls: My grandmother was born in Budapest in September 1932, and she still remembers the peaceful and relaxed atmosphere of the Friday evenings of her then-happy childhood. She recognized Shabbat by the smell of challah spreading through the house. Her mother and grandmother woke up very early to prepare all the food: gefilte fish, chicken soup with noodles, meat, cake, and compote. The festive evenings with the whole family were wonderful. And along with her little brother, she loved even more the one day of the week when they had a "doughy lunch." After the soup, these fine and tasty plum dumplings would appear on the table.

Eva recalls: Once, when we came home from synagogue on Rosh Hashanah, my parents asked me to watch my little three-year-old brother, Tamás, while they went to rest a bit. Since Tamás was particularly quiet, I thought he was looking at his picture books. Way too late, I noticed that Tamás discovered the big pot of plum jam for the plum dumplings and ate from it with pleasure. It must have tasted good to him, because he was covered from head to toe with jam. I was scared that I would get scolded, but when our parents came downstairs everyone laughed. Then I helped him wash off the delicious jam in the bathtub. In the evening, Tamás didn't need any dinner, because the tub was almost empty, and he was full.

YIELDS ABOUT 6–8 DUMPLINGS

- 2 pounds small purple plums
- Sugar cubes, to replace the pit of each plum
- Ground cinnamon, for sprinkling
- 1½ cups all-purpose flour, sifted, plus more for rolling

Wash and pit the plums. Put a sugar cube in each piece and sprinkle with cinnamon. Set aside.

Add the flour, salt, butter, and egg yolk to the cooled mashed potatoes and knead to form a dough. On a floured work surface, roll the dough out about ⅓ inch thick and cut into 2-inch squares. Place a prepared plum in the middle of each square and roll into a ball. Bring a pot of salted water to a boil over medium-high heat and cook the dumplings until they rise to the surface, 7 to 8 minutes.

¼ teaspoon salt, plus more for cooking the dumplings
1 tablespoon butter
1 egg yolk
1¼ pounds potatoes, boiled, mashed, and cooled
4–5 tablespoons unseasoned bread crumbs
1 tablespoon vegetable oil
Powdered sugar, for finishing

Remove with a slotted spoon or sieve and place in a colander to drain.

In the meantime, toast the bread crumbs with the oil in a large frying pan or in the oven for 5 minutes. Roll the cooked dumplings in the bread crumbs and dust with powdered sugar and cinnamon to serve.

Note: The best kind of potatoes for this recipe are floury ones.

COLD STRAWBERRY SOUP

Survivor | **EVA KERENYI**

Eva's son John recalls: This was my mom's spin on an old family cherry soup recipe. She experimented with the original recipe and came up with the strawberry soup recipe on her own. This recipe was a summer favorite growing up. My mom used to make it for us on long, warm days. I remember being called inside by her after playing on a hot summer's evening and having this tasty and refreshing soup as a starter for dinner. It's always best served cold. The combination of wine, sour cream, and strawberries tasted like my childhood. The red wine somehow brings out the flavors of the dish. You can't taste the red wine on its own, but it's vital for enhancing the strawberry flavor. It's a refreshing and perfect combination!

SERVES 2–4 AS A MAIN DISH OR 6 AS AN APPETIZER OR SIDE DISH

2 pounds fresh strawberries, stems and leaves removed
¾ cup red wine, or more as needed
¾ cup sour cream, or more as needed
½ cup sugar, or to taste

Roughly chop the strawberries and place in a blender. Add the wine, sour cream, and sugar, and blend until smooth. Thin the mixture with additional wine or sour cream, if needed. Serve chilled.

Note: You do not strain the soup. You blend it, and the seeds are part of the soup's taste and texture.

COLD CHERRY SOUP WITH EGG-WHITE DUMPLINGS

Survivor | **ANNELIESE NOSSBAUM**

Anneliese's children, Jeffrey, Jan, and Eileen, recall that this cherry soup was Anneliese's favorite recipe for hot summer days.

The dumplings on the soup are made from egg whites, like meringues. They are like sweet little clouds floating on top of the colorful soup. It's a perfect pairing of light sweetness and tartness of the fruit that sinks into the bottom of the bowl.

Anneliese's family considers this recipe special because they have always made it for summer Shabbat dinners. Part of her family's Shabbat dinner tradition is soup. It is just too hot to sit down to a steaming bowl of soup in the summertime, so this soup came out on those warm evenings, something they looked forward to all winter long.

SERVES 8

FOR THE SOUP:

2 cups cherry juice
2 cups plus 2 tablespoons water
Juice of 1 lemon
2 tablespoons cornstarch
24-ounce jar (or two 13-ounce cans) pitted sour cherries with juice
Up to ½ cup sugar

FOR THE DUMPLINGS:

2 egg whites
2 cups water
2 tablespoons sugar
Grated lemon peel (optional)

Make the soup: In a small saucepan, bring the cherry juice, 2 cups water, and lemon juice to a boil over high heat. In a small bowl, whisk the cornstarch with the remaining 2 tablespoons water to make a slurry. Add to the saucepan, whisking to dissolve. Add the cherries with their juices. Taste and add sugar, a little at a time, until the soup reaches desired sweetness. Boil for 2 minutes more, or until the sugar dissolves. Cool at room temperature, then refrigerate to chill thoroughly.

Make the dumplings: In a large bowl, beat the egg whites to soft peaks. Fill a saucepan with water, add the sugar and lemon peel, if using, and bring to a simmer over medium heat. Working in batches, dollop tablespoons of egg whites into the sugar water. Cook until set on one side, 1 to 2 minutes, then flip and cook until firm on the other side. Remove the dumplings with a slotted spoon and put them directly into the soup. Serve cold.

COLD STRING-BEAN SOUP

(Yiddish: intergeshlugeneh zup)

Survivor | **LOIS FLAMHOLZ**

I like to make this soup with fresh beans—fresh summer produce makes the flavor better. But you can make it any time of year.

SERVES 4

6 cups water
1 teaspoon salt, or to taste
12–16 ounces string (green) beans, trimmed
1 tablespoon white vinegar
2 eggs
½ cup heavy cream

Pour the water into a large pot and add the salt. Bring to a boil over high heat. Cut the string beans into pieces and cook until soft. Remove the green beans to a colander, reserving the cooking water in the pot. Add the vinegar to the pot.

In a medium bowl, beat together the eggs and cream. Gradually add to the cooking water, whisking it in quickly and continuously so the eggs don't curdle. Return the string beans to the soup. Cool completely, then transfer to a container and refrigerate until cold, at least 1 hour. Taste and season with more salt if needed.

BORSCHT

Survivor | **LOIS FLAMHOLZ**

This is a healthy and nutritious soup that is perfect for the fall.

SERVES 4–5

3 potatoes
2 carrots
2 celery ribs
1 red bell pepper
1 onion
3 beets
5 tablespoons olive oil
8 cups chicken broth
4 tablespoons tomato sauce
2 bay leaves
1 garlic clove, smashed
2 tablespoons chopped fresh dill, plus additional fronds for serving
Salt and pepper, to taste
Sour cream, for serving (optional)

Peel and slice the potatoes and carrots. Finely chop the celery, bell pepper, and onion. Peel and grate the beets (or slice them if you prefer).

Heat a large pot over medium heat, add 3 tablespoons of the olive oil and the beets. When the beets soften, add the chicken broth and 2 cups water, as well as the potatoes and carrots. Cook until all of the vegetables are soft.

At the same time, heat a second large pot over medium heat. Add the remaining 2 tablespoons of olive oil with the celery, bell pepper, and onion. When they all become golden brown, add the tomato sauce and stir-fry for up to 1 minute. Transfer the sautéed vegetables to the pot with the soup and continue cooking.

Add the bay leaves, garlic, and chopped dill. Add salt and pepper to taste. Simmer for 1 to 2 minutes. Garnish each serving with dill and sour cream if you like.

DAVID'S SHLISHKES

Survivor | **DAVID MARKS**

Shlishkes, sometimes known as shlishkas, are a potato dumpling popular in Hungarian-Jewish households. They can be served savory or sweet, rolled in seasoned bread crumbs or cinnamon and sugar. They make a great appetizer or a delicious snack. My family loves them, and my oldest sister, Manci, taught me a great trick on preparing this dish quickly for the whole family. She admitted that she made it in large batches and froze it once it was rolled out and cut (she would roll it in more flour to prevent it from sticking together when frozen). She would take it out of the freezer, cook it in boiling water, and roll it in crispy, toasted bread crumbs.

SERVES 5

About 5 medium potatoes, unpeeled
2 large eggs, beaten
About 1½ cups all-purpose flour, plus more for rolling
3 tablespoons vegetable oil, plus more for rolling
Dash of salt
1 cup unseasoned bread crumbs

Place the potatoes in a pot with water to cover by a few inches. Bring to a boil over high heat. Drain and let the potatoes cool completely. Peel the potatoes, place them in a large bowl, and mash them well.

Make a large well in the middle of the mashed potatoes and pour in the eggs. Gradually pull the walls of the potato well into the eggs and mix well. Start adding the flour in small increments until the mixture can no longer absorb any more. Knead well and add 2 tablespoons of the oil and the salt to the dough.

Bring a pot of water to a boil while you form the dumplings and preheat the broiler.

Flour a work surface. Coat your hands with oil, take a piece of the dough, and roll it into a long strand about ¾ inch thick. Cut the strand into ¾-inch slices. Working in batches to avoid crowding the pot, add the slices of shlishkes to the water and cook until the dumplings rise to the surface, gently nudging them off the sides of the pot if they begin to stick. Cook for another 5 minutes.

While the dumplings are cooking, heat the remaining 1 tablespoon oil in a medium skillet over medium heat. Add the bread crumbs and toast, stirring, until browned.

Drain the shlishkes and gently toss them in the toasted bread crumbs. Transfer to a broiler pan, place under the broiler, and broil until golden brown.

Shlishkes can also be made without breading and paired with sauce instead. To freeze, roll the shlishkes in flour before boiling them and place in a zip-top bag.

Note: Yukon Gold potatoes work the best with this recipe. The bread crumbs should be toasted to a crispy brown and—if desired—seasoned as well.

LEA'S SHLISHKES

Survivor | **LEA ROTH**

When I have company or when it's Shavuot, I make a special food called shlishkes. Americans call it gnocchi. Each country has some variation of this. At home, the way I made it was with bread crumbs—fry the crumbs, put them on top—or add hazelnuts and sugar. I became well known for my shlishkes. Recently, I made this dish for an engagement party, and we also had some from the bakery. People tasted both, and everyone agreed that the homemade shlishkes were better. They are simply delicious.

I make two variations of this recipe. Sometimes I use eggs, and sometimes not. Within the last ten years, Tziporah, my friend from the war with whom I reunited later in Israel, told me not to use eggs because the shlishkes come out fluffier.

SERVES 8

5 large potatoes, peeled and cut into eighths
Pinch of salt, plus more for cooking the potatoes
2 eggs
3 cups all-purpose flour, plus more for the work surface

FOR SERVING:

Butter, margarine, or oil with bread crumbs or grated cheese and spices (for savory shlishkes)
Sugar and ground nuts, such as hazelnuts (for sweet shlishkes)

Cook the potatoes in boiling salted water until soft. Drain them and mash until smooth. Set aside to cool slightly.

While the potatoes are cooling, prepare a fresh pot of boiling water, filled about halfway.

In a large bowl, add the mashed potatoes and the eggs and mix to combine, then incorporate the flour.

Prepare a clean, dry surface with some additional flour. Place a handful of the potato mixture onto the floured surface and roll it into a snake with the palm of your hand. Cut each roll into uniform 2- to 3-inch pieces. Repeat with the remainder of the mixture.

Drop the cut pieces into the boiling water. They will sink to the bottom and then float to the top. Cook for about 5 minutes, then remove with a large slotted spoon.

There are many ways to prepare accompaniments for the shlishkes: I prefer frying them in bread crumbs with a little bit of butter (for dairy) or oil or margarine (for parve). Another suggestion is to put them in a container with a little bit of oil or melted butter to keep them from sticking.

For a sweet preparation, roll the shlishkes in a mixture

of sugar and ground nuts. For savory, a mixture of melted butter and grated cheese with spices can be added to the cooked shlishkes. Be creative and experiment with any ingredients you like.

Note: Russet potatoes make the best shlishkes. If you want to finish the shlishkes with cheese, Lea recommends mozzarella cheese, cheddar, or a mix.

CHEESE DUMPLINGS

Survivor | **EVA SHAINBLUM**

The cheese dumplings recipe has been our family's favorite Shavuot dish since I was a little girl. It has been passed down from generation to generation in an oral form. It has not changed at all, even though I have never written it down. All of the quantities are estimates from my memory.

My children loved these dumplings too (my daughter Esther likes it served without the crumbs). What makes this dish particularly delicious is its sweetness and lightness. It is a perfect dish for the summer. It can be served as the main dairy dish or as a sweet side dish.

SERVES 4–6

2 eggs, beaten
2 tablespoons granulated sugar
1 pound farmer cheese or dry cottage cheese
About ½ cup semolina or cream of wheat
2 tablespoons vanilla sugar or 2 teaspoons vanilla extract
¾ cup white bread crumbs
Vegetable oil
Salt
Zest of 1 lemon
1 cup sour cream or yogurt, if preferred

Beat the eggs and granulated sugar together. Crumble the cheese into a large bowl and mix in the egg mixture, semolina or cream of wheat, and vanilla sugar. Set aside for 20 minutes.

Meanwhile, toast the bread crumbs with a small amount of oil in a frying pan over high heat. Pour into a large bowl or onto a baking sheet and set aside to cool.

To cook the dumplings, bring a pot of salted water to a boil. Using your hands, shape the cheese mixture into small balls and carefully drop them into the boiling water. Reduce the heat to medium and cook, uncovered, until the dumplings rise to the surface. Remove with a slotted spoon and roll them in the toasted bread crumbs. Serve topped with the lemon zest and sour cream.

Note: The consistency of the egg, sugar, and cheese mixture must be thick enough to hold the shape of a ball. It is best to use dry pressed cottage cheese, not curds. You add the cream of wheat dry and uncooked to the cottage cheese as a binding agent.

PATENTED
Dec. 16, 1969
3,484,114
SCREW INSTALLING ATTACH
POWER TOOLS
FIG. 1.

MAIN DISHES

מנות עיקריות

STUFFED CABBAGE WITH SAUERKRAUT

(Yiddish: holishkes)

Survivor | **DAVID MARKS**

When my mother made stuffed cabbage, it signaled a special event or a holiday. This feeling has stayed with me since, and—until this day—cooking this meal puts me in a celebratory mood. The bed of ingredients and the roll with the meat and rice plus the added seasonings make it just too moist and tasty. It is time-consuming to make but so delicious. I always make too much. I usually give some to neighbors or, better yet, freeze for a meal in the future.

Over the years, I have embellished my mother's original recipe with V8 juice and Heinz Chili Sauce. Of course, when I was a child, all of the ingredients were fresh and homemade. Now I use some canned items like tomato paste. However, when it comes to the sauerkraut, I always make and ferment it myself. You can also buy organic sauerkraut in health-food stores or grocery stores.

SERVES 4–6

1 medium green cabbage
1 large onion, half minced and half thinly sliced
1 pound ground beef
½ cup dried white rice
1 large egg, lightly beaten
2½ cups chicken stock
1 teaspoon freshly ground black pepper
1 pound fresh sauerkraut (not canned), slightly drained
¼ cup tomato paste
28-ounce can crushed tomatoes

Preheat the oven to 350°F (for a faster bake) or 200°F (for a slower simmer).

Use a sharp knife to cut out the central hard core of the cabbage. In a large pot, bring 6 quarts water to a boil over high heat. Carefully drop the biggest outer leaves of the cabbage into the boiling water. Boil until the leaves are soft. After 2 minutes, remove the leaves to a large platter to cool.

Shred the remainder of the cabbage and set aside.

Sauté the minced onion until tender. In a large bowl, combine the sautéed onion, beef, rice, egg, ½ cup of the chicken stock, and pepper. Set aside.

In a second large bowl, toss the shredded cabbage, sliced onion, and sauerkraut.

In a third large bowl, whisk the tomato paste and the crushed tomatoes with the remaining 2 cups stock.

On the bottom of a 6-quart casserole dish or Dutch oven, spread half of the sauerkraut mixture to make a bed for the cabbage rolls. Evenly spoon half of the tomato mixture over the sauerkraut mixture.

To stuff the cabbage, place a cabbage leaf in front of you with the stem end facing down and away from you. Place a scoop of the meat and rice mixture in the middle of the leaf. Fold the bottom (stem end) of the leaf down toward the top of the leaf, then fold the right side inward and over toward the left. Fold down the top of the leaf and push the left edge inside to create a pocket. You want the package to have some space in it for the rice to swell as it cooks. Place the roll seam side down into the prepared casserole dish or Dutch oven. Repeat until you have stuffed all the cabbage leaves and filled the dish with one layer of stuffed cabbage. Spread the remaining sauerkraut mixture and the remaining tomato mixture on top.

Bake until the sauce is bubbling, about 30 minutes. Cover the baking dish with foil or place the lid on the Dutch oven and continue cooking for 5 hours at 350°F or 8 hours at 200°F.

Note: I did not include any salt in the recipe. I generally let people salt their food, since many diets require low sodium and everyone's taste is different. The result is better if you cook it at a lower temperature for longer to let the flavors simmer and combine. You can use a slow cooker, but I find the flavors taste best when cooked in the oven. I sometimes take a little of the beef mixture and fry and taste it to see if more garlic or salt is needed.

SWEET-AND-SOUR STUFFED CABBAGE

(Yiddish: holishkes)

Survivor | **LOIS FLAMHOLZ**

In the 1930s, the Bronx was the most Jewish borough of New York City, with almost 50 percent of the population identifying as Jewish. That is where Lois moved when she first arrived in the United States. This version of stuffed cabbage—relying for its zing on such supermarket staples as ginger ale and ketchup—was particularly popular among the blossoming Jewish Bronx community.

SERVES 6–8

1 medium green cabbage
1 liter ginger ale
32-ounce bottle ketchup
1 large onion, diced
2 tablespoons olive oil
2 pounds ground beef
½ cup cooked brown or white rice
1 apple, grated (optional)
Salt and pepper, or other seasoning, to taste

Separate cabbage leaves and add to boiling water to soften, about 20 minutes.

In an 8-quart pot, add ginger ale and ketchup and boil for 15 minutes. Meanwhile, sauté the diced onion in a little olive oil.

In a large bowl, combine the ground beef, rice, and sautéed onion. If desired, add a grated apple. Season to taste. Divide the mixture into medium-size balls. Place each one in a cabbage leaf and fold over to seal. Simmer in the ketchup and ginger ale mixture, uncovered, for 1½ hours.

CHOLENT WITH EGGS AND KISHKE

(Yiddish: tsholnt)

Survivor | **DAVID LENGA**

To have cholent in a Yiddish home, in prewar Poland, in Łódź, was a must. There was no Shabbat without the cholent. It's just the way it was. Everybody looked forward to it. It was the taste of heaven. When I was a ten- or eleven-year-old boy, my mother would put all the cholent ingredients into a black cast-iron pot. She would wrap it around very tight with paper and then with string. She would wrap it hermetically tight. She would put a lid on it and then give it to me—the oldest boy—to go to the neighborhood bakery. The baker would put it in his oven and give you the top part of a ticket. Part of the ticket with the number would go on the cholent, and the other part you would hold on to and redeem your food later. And so I went every Friday before Shabbat to the baker to take the cholent for the family. All the other Jews were doing the same thing. There were hundreds of people lined up outside of the baker's store: the whole neighborhood. Everybody did it.

SERVES 8–12

1 cup dried beans: lima, pinto, red (not kidney), or a mixture (see notes)
2½ pounds large red potatoes, peeled and halved (for smaller slow cooker, use 2 pounds)
2 yellow onions, chopped
2½ pounds beef stew meat or brisket, cut into chunks (for smaller slow cooker, use 2 pounds)
2 marrowbones

Presoak the beans: Place the beans into the bottom of a large pot and cover with several inches of water. (The beans will double in size as they soak, so make sure to use plenty of water.) Boil for 5 minutes, then remove the pot from the heat. Let soak for 1 hour, then drain and rinse well before proceeding with the recipe.

Make the stew: In a large slow cooker (the larger the better!), place the potatoes in a single layer on the bottom of the cooking vessel. Sprinkle the onions over the potatoes. Place the beef in a single layer on top of the vegetables and add the marrowbones. (If you're adding kishke, now would be the time to put it in the cooker.)

Rinse the beans, checking for any stones or impurities. If using barley or kasha, do the same with the grains. Sprinkle the beans and grains, if you choose, over the top

1 kishke (optional, see note; we never add this, but many families like it)
½ cup pearl barley or coarse-grain kasha (optional; for a gluten-free version, use kasha)
3 cloves garlic, peeled
½ teaspoon ground black pepper, or to taste
6 eggs (optional)
4 cups low-sodium chicken broth
1 tablespoon kosher salt
1½ teaspoons paprika
1½ teaspoons ground turmeric
1 teaspoon ground cumin
¼ teaspoon cayenne (if spice-sensitive, use just a pinch)

of the meat. Tuck the garlic cloves into the meat, spacing them evenly. Sprinkle black pepper over the top. If using eggs, rinse their shells well and then tuck them into the meat.

Put the broth in a container and whisk in the salt, paprika, turmeric, cumin, and cayenne. Pour the liquid over the cholent. Add additional water until all the beans and pieces of meat are covered, approximately another 1 to 2 cups (it may vary depending on the slow cooker; I usually add a bit more liquid if using grains, because they will soak it up).

Cover the slow cooker and cook on low power for 16 hours, checking occasionally and adding water if the mixture looks dry. When the cooking is complete, most cookers will auto-switch to warm. If yours doesn't, set it to warm until ready to serve. Peel the eggs (if using) before serving.

The cholent will look a bit medieval when it's done cooking! Don't worry, just dig in and you'll see that it's perfectly cooked below the surface.

Notes: A 6- to 8-quart slow cooker is recommended for this recipe, but it can also be cooked in a low oven for 12 to 16 hours. The beans in this recipe will soften without any presoaking due to the long slow-cooking process, but they will be easier to digest with a simple, quick soak before cooking. It is not recommended to slow-cook kidney beans. Kishke is a sausage made with flour and often flavored with chicken fat and onion. It can be ordered from specialty delicatessens.

cholent

2 pounds flanken cut into 2 inch pieces
1/2 cup large lima beans dried
1/2 " barley
2-3 pounds red potatoes cut into chunks
3 large onions chopped saute until light brown
salt & pepper to taste
mix everything together
cover with water
bake in a 300° degree oven covered
overnight. The cholent should be moist
without extra liquid.

CHOLENT

(Yiddish: tsholnt)

Survivor | **ROSALIE SIMON**

Cholent was a traditional Shabbos lunch. When the people came back from synagogue, we used to pick up the cholent from the bakery, and everybody sat around the table and had the chopped liver and the cholent. This was a favorite of most of the people because you are not allowed to cook on Shabbos or heat up food, so that's what we did. It came out hot from the oven, and it was delicious.

During the war, at the factory in Geislinge an der Steige, Germany, we did not have enough to eat. We got a little coffee in the morning and a little slice of bread. We had some soup for lunch, which was better than Auschwitz, but we were hungry all the time. For the night, we had two little rotten potatoes, and I thought to myself, "I only want one thing in my life: I want to get out of here. I want to get liberated, and I simply want enough potatoes in my life. That's it. I don't want anything else in my life."

SERVES 10

3 large onions, chopped
2 pounds flanken, cut into 2-inch pieces
½ cup dried large lima beans, rinsed and picked over
½ cup barley, rinsed and picked over
2–3 pounds red potatoes, cut into chunks
Salt and black pepper

Preheat the oven to 300°F.

Sauté onions until light brown and combine with all other ingredients in a large Dutch oven or casserole dish. Cover with water and bake, covered, overnight. The cholent should be moist without extra liquid.

BRISKET

Survivor | **GOLDIE FINKELSTEIN**

Goldie's son Joe remembers: The story of my mother and food has many psychological layers. Her recipes are not what she learned as a child, but they are the product of what she experienced as a child and how she didn't want the same experience to be her children's. She connected food and feeding to life and survival. She was pretty well known in town for her food. A lot of people came over, and she gave away as much as she could.

SERVES 4–8, DEPENDING ON BRISKET SIZE

FOR THE MEAT:

1 medium brisket (about 8 ounces per person)
2–4 tablespoons vegetable oil, plus more to rub on the brisket
Salt
Garlic powder
Paprika
2–4 onions, sliced
1 envelope (2 ounces) French onion soup mix (optional; see note)

FOR THE GRAVY:

Liquid from the cooked brisket
Flour
Garlic powder
Black pepper

Preheat the oven to 350°F. Rinse the brisket with cold water and pat dry. Rub with a light coating of oil and salt, garlic powder, and paprika.

Add enough oil to cover the bottom of a Dutch oven or other oven-safe pot and heat over high heat. Sear the brisket on each side, until well browned all over. Remove the pot from the heat.

Remove the brisket from the pot and place onions on the bottom of the pot. Place the brisket back in the pot and sprinkle the onion soup mix on top, if using.

Cover and bake, checking the pot for liquid after 30 minutes. If there is no liquid, add a little water. Continue cooking until a meat thermometer reads at least 170°F, about 3 to 4 hours. Once cooked, remove the brisket and onions, leaving behind the cooking liquid.

Place the pot back on the stove top. Skim the fat from the liquid and add cold water, if needed. Add a little flour to thicken, plus garlic powder and pepper to taste. Cook gravy over medium heat until reduced.

Let the brisket rest on a carving board for a few minutes. To serve, slice across the grain and add gravy to taste. Can be stored overnight in the refrigerator in a covered container.

Note: For Passover, omit the dry onion soup mix (if you can't find a Passover-safe version) and substitute potato starch for the flour.

CRISPY MEAT PATTIES

(Hungarian: fasìrt)

Survivor | **DAVID MARKS**

I have so many favorite meals inspired by my childhood that I often make with pride and memories today. Last week, I made Hungarian-style stuffed cabbage with plenty of sauerkraut. This week, I made cholent with lots of beans, barley, beef brisket, potatoes, and onions. I will make fasìrt, mini meatloaf hamburgers that are fried, and wide-cut fresh pasta noodles tossed with sugar and ground walnuts or pecans. There were so many delicious delights in my childhood that took a lot of work then, but that I enjoy making so quickly today. If only my sweet mother and adoring sisters could see me now!

SERVES 4

1 pound lean ground beef (90/10)
¾ cup finely chopped sweet onion
2 large cloves garlic, finely chopped
2 eggs
½ cup seasoned bread crumbs
½ teaspoon salt
½ teaspoon ground black pepper
3 tablespoons ketchup or chili ketchup
3 tablespoons vegetable oil

In a large bowl, combine the beef, onion, garlic, eggs, bread crumbs, salt and pepper, and ketchup. Form small, round patties about the size of a silver dollar.

Heat the oil in a large cast-iron skillet over medium-low heat, add the patties, and cook for 7 to 8 minutes per side. Carefully splash a few drops of cold water into the pan, cover, and steam the patties for 2 to 3 minutes. Serve hot with vegetables. (They are also very good eaten cold the following day!)

HUNGARIAN GOULASH

Survivor | **EVA SZEPESI**

I am happy every time my grandchildren and great-grandchildren are visiting me. And they are always excited when I cook pörkölt with nokedli. I love when they all eat with joy. In this way, I can pass on to them a little bit of our Hungarian roots.

My memory of this meal goes back to the time before the war. My mom and grandma used to make it for our family. As a child, I especially loved the homemade nokedli that came with the goulash. After Auschwitz, my aunt and mother-in-law cooked it. Luckily, the taste didn't change much because the ingredients remained very similar. After the war, I took over the recipe from my aunt and my mother-in-law because—unfortunately—my mother was no longer with us to continue the family tradition of cooking it. I saw my mother for the last time when I was eleven years old.

When it comes to the size of the dumplings, I recommend dividing the dough into strips, cutting small pieces with a knife, and then dropping them directly into the boiling water in the pot. The smaller the pieces are, the more delicious the nokedli will be.

This dish is particularly appetizing due to its deep red color and the excellent taste of the sweet Hungarian paprika powder.

SERVES 4–6

FOR THE GOULASH:

2 tablespoons vegetable oil
2 large onions, sliced
1 pound boneless beef shoulder, cut into bite-size chunks
1 red bell pepper, chopped
1 yellow bell pepper, chopped
2 tomatoes, sliced
1 tablespoon tomato paste
2 teaspoons sweet Hungarian paprika
1½ teaspoons salt

Make the goulash: Heat the oil in a large Dutch oven over medium heat. Add the onions and cook until they start to soften. Increase the heat to medium-high, add the beef, and brown on all sides. Add the red and yellow peppers, the tomatoes, tomato paste, paprika, salt, and ½ cup water. Bring to a simmer, then cover, reduce the heat to low, and cook for about 2 hours, until the beef is tender. Lift the lid a few times to stir and add more water if the pot is looking dry.

FOR THE DUMPLINGS (NOKEDLI):

¼ teaspoon salt, plus more for the cooking water
1 cup all-purpose flour
2 eggs
Up to ½ cup cold water
Vegetable oil, for finishing

Make the dumplings: Set a large saucepan of salted water to boil over medium-high heat.

In a large bowl, whisk the flour and salt. Stir in the eggs using a wooden spoon and add just enough water to make a soft, sticky dough.

Grate or cut the dough into small pieces and drop them into the boiling water. After the nokedli rise to the surface, cook for an additional 2 minutes. Drizzle the oil over the nokedli and serve immediately with the goulash.

VEAL PAPRIKASH

(Hungarian: paprikás)

Survivor | **ALEXANDER SPILBERG**

Before the war, my family could not afford to get veal, so this dish was not something we could make. I learned how to cook it when I moved to Canada. It is a particularly delicious dish that has become my family's favorite. All the kids love it.

SERVES 4–8

3 tablespoons vegetable oil
2 medium (or 1 large) onions, chopped
1 teaspoon paprika
1½ pounds veal shoulder steak, cut into small cubes
2 teaspoons all-purpose seasoning blend
1 cup boiling water, plus more as needed
1 teaspoon chopped fresh parsley
2 plum tomatoes, peeled and chopped
1 teaspoon salt
1 carrot, cut into bite-size pieces
4 medium boiling potatoes, cut into bite-size pieces

Heat the oil in a large Dutch oven over medium heat. Add the onion and paprika and cook, stirring occasionally until the onion is golden brown. Add the veal shoulder, then add the seasoning blend and continue cooking, stirring occasionally for a few minutes. Add the boiling water and cook, stirring frequently, then add the parsley, tomatoes, and salt.

Bring to a simmer, then reduce the heat, cover, and simmer for about 1½ hours, checking periodically and adding more boiling water as needed, until the meat is just about tender. Add the carrot and potatoes and some additional boiling water and cook for 30 minutes, or until the potatoes are cooked through. Serve.

Note: We would typically pair this dish with a salad that we would serve first.

TURKEY AND STUFFING

Survivor | **RUTH WEBBER**

When it comes to the quantity of each vegetable or fruit listed in the ingredients list, I only focus on how much I can fit in the cavity of the turkey. Usually, I cut up one orange, one apple, one onion, a few stalks of celery, and carrots (cut into 3-inch pieces). Fit as much as you can into the cavity—and eat the rest for lunch!

Additionally, when it comes to garlic and spices, I usually use a head or two of garlic, depending on how much garlic you like! As for the spices, start with a teaspoon of each and adjust to your taste. Some people like a lot more paprika, which gives a nice color to the rub and the skin.

SERVES 12–15

16-pound turkey
½ cup vegetable oil, plus more if needed
⅓ cup minced garlic
2 tablespoons paprika
2 teaspoons ground black pepper
2 teaspoons salt
2 carrots
2 large stalks celery
1 large apple
1 large orange, peeled
1 large yellow onion

Clean the turkey well, inside and out. In a medium bowl, whisk the oil with the garlic, paprika, black pepper, and salt to make a paste. Spread it over the turkey, making sure to get under the skin (without tearing it) and inside the cavity and neck area as much as possible. Wrap the turkey in aluminum foil and refrigerate overnight.

One hour before roasting, remove the turkey from the refrigerator and allow it to rest uncovered.

While the turkey is resting, preheat the oven to 325°F.

Cut the carrots, celery, apple, orange, and onion into chunks and mix together. Stuff into the cavity of the turkey until full, then close with foil or a skewer.

Before placing the turkey into the roasting pan, take a long sheet of aluminum foil and fold it to create a long strip, about 3 inches wide. Lay it across the pan lengthwise, so that it comes up the sides of the pan and overlaps the edges. This will help when removing the turkey after roasting.

Put the turkey into the roasting pan and secure the wings to the breasts with skewers, to protect the breasts from burning. Tie the *pulkes* (legs) together with string or a skewer. If the turkey is very dry, add more oil to keep the breast from drying out.

Roast for 3½ hours, checking for browning on the wings and legs after 1 hour. Wrap with aluminum foil if the turkey starts to burn. After another 30 minutes, or when the breast begins to look done, tent the meat with aluminum foil (the foil should cover the turkey without touching it, to allow room to breathe). When removing the roasting pan from the oven, tighten the tent onto the turkey. Allow the turkey to rest, covered with a foil tent or kitchen towels, to keep warm until carving.

Note: The ingredient quantities in this recipe are to taste and can be easily adjusted according to the size of your turkey. Make sure you plan for the overnight spice rub.

CHICKEN PAPRIKASH

(Hungarian: paprikás csirke)

Survivor | **DAVID MARKS**

After my wife died, I had to learn how to cook. I had all my sisters in Israel, excellent cooks, and they wrote in Hebrew and Hungarian recipes for me. I went to visit them, and they taught me. I came home and fell in love with cooking. I cook like I make furniture because my trade is to make furniture. So, I design it. I design the food. I buy the lumber—I purchase the potatoes, onions. When everything is ready, I put it together.

SERVES 2–4

2 tablespoons olive oil
2 chicken legs
2 chicken thighs
Salt
2 large yellow onions, sliced
2–4 tablespoons sweet paprika
Black pepper
Cayenne pepper
1 cup chicken broth
¼ cup sour cream
Cooked rice, for serving

Heat the olive oil in a large sauté pan over high heat. Season the chicken with salt and cook until browned on all sides. Remove the chicken from the pan to a plate. Add the onions to the pan, lower the heat to medium, and cook, stirring often, until well browned. Stir in the paprika, to taste, and season with black pepper and cayenne. Pour in the chicken broth and stir well. Nestle the chicken on top of the onions. Cover, lower the heat to maintain a low simmer, and cook for about 20 to 25 minutes, until the chicken is cooked through. Remove the chicken from the pan and stir sour cream into the onions. Serve the chicken and onion mixture over rice.

CHICKEN SCHNITZEL

Survivor | **GOLDIE FINKELSTEIN**

Goldie's son Joe remembers that this meal was served every Rosh Hashanah dinner, in addition to brisket and a turkey. Everyone knew that Goldie would serve three entrees, maybe seven side dishes, and multiple desserts.

SERVES 4

1 pound chicken cutlets
1 cup all-purpose flour
Salt and black pepper
2 large eggs, beaten
1½ cups cornflake crumbs
¼ cup sliced or slivered almonds
Vegetable oil, for the pan

Pound chicken cutlets to desired thinness. Dredge in flour, salt, and pepper. Dredge in beaten eggs. Coat breasts on both sides with cornflake crumbs mixed with almond slices. Shallow fry in oil till lightly browned on both sides. Remove and place on a cookie sheet. Bake in oven at 375°F till fully done, about 10 minutes. Serve.

CRUSTED SWEET CHICKEN

Survivor | **RACHEL ROTH**

At Majdanek, Rachel and the other women in her barrack were forced to witness the hanging of a young girl. In her book, Rachel recalled diverting everyone's attention from this horrific incident by telling other women stories about what a Friday night was like in her house in Warsaw before the war. "To divert our attention from the gallows and shorten the endless night, I tried to create a picture of the wonderful family atmosphere for my depressed listeners," she wrote. "With great respect, Father removes two fresh shiny challahs from a white napkin embroidered with colorful thread. We thank our Creator for the bread we have cultivated from the earth. The white, soft challah gives off an inviting aroma. Father cuts it into large pieces, which he distributes to the family." Rachel emphasized the food, as the purpose of her story was to conjure up the taste and smell of the wonderful meal, hoping that this would relieve her friends' hunger. "Well-baked chicken skin crunches under our teeth. The delicious compote retains the taste of fresh fruit." Rachel noticed that there was no further praying, crying, or moaning as she told her story. "All is silent. We cling to each other, trying to warm each other with our bodies. The girls listen attentively to my story from the thousand and one nights. They have forgotten about their hunger and the girl on the gallows."

SERVES 4–6

FOR THE CHICKEN:

1 box soup nuts or mandlen (oyster) crackers, crushed

1 teaspoon ground ginger

½ teaspoon garlic powder

½ teaspoon salt

½ teaspoon black pepper

2 large eggs

1 teaspoon fresh lemon juice

1 pound boneless, skinless chicken breasts or thighs

FOR THE GLAZE:

½ cup white wine

2 tablespoons margarine, melted

2 cups duck sauce

¼ teaspoon ground ginger

¼ teaspoon ground cloves

1 tablespoon honey

Prepare the chicken: Preheat the oven to 400°F and prepare a large casserole dish or sturdy baking pan with nonstick cooking spray.

Using a mortar and pestle or food processor, crush together the soup nuts and the ginger, garlic powder, salt, and pepper. Pour onto a large plate. In a shallow dish, beat the eggs with the lemon juice. Dip each piece of chicken into the egg mixture, followed by the crumbs, then arrange the chicken pieces in the prepared casserole dish. Set aside.

Make the glaze: In a microwave-safe bowl, combine the wine, margarine, duck sauce, ginger, cloves, and honey and heat slowly in the microwave to reach a smooth pouring consistency. Pour the glaze over the chicken, then bake in the preheated oven for 1 hour, or until cooked through.

NOODLES WITH POPPY SEEDS

(Hungarian: mákos tészta)

Survivor | **EVA SZEPESI**

One of my favorite memories associated with this dish is getting pleasantly sleepy after eating it. I would often fall asleep on the couch right after finishing the meal. Many Hungarian children loved this simple and sweet dish. While it is sweet, my family always served it as the main dish with no side dishes to go with it. The only exception was putting some extra poppy seeds mixed with sugar on the table if someone wanted more on the noodles. That is also how I have always served it. My children, grandchildren, and great-grandchildren also love it. It is sweet and straightforward.

This recipe has not changed over the years. It is precisely the way we used to make it in Hungary. The only difference is the type of noodles: it is hard to get flat Hungarian noodles abroad. So you need to improvise and use similar ones. After the war, when family or friends came to visit us from Hungary, they always brought us flat noodles.

When it comes to the time needed to cook the pasta, it all depends on the thickness of the noodles you are using. We always used flat noodles because the poppy seeds stuck to them better.

SERVES 8

- 14 ounces noodles (wide-strip pasta like tagliatelle or szélesmetélt)
- Salt, for cooking the pasta
- 7 ounces ground poppy seeds
- 2 cups powdered sugar or honey
- 3½ tablespoons butter

Cook the pasta in a large pot of salted water according to the package instructions until tender. Drain.

Mix the ground poppy seeds and powdered sugar in a bowl.

Melt the butter in a large sauté pan over medium heat. Transfer the noodles to the pan, toss to coat with butter, and cook for 1 to 2 minutes. Remove from heat and add the sweetened poppy seeds to the pasta. Toss to combine.

KASHA VARNISHKES

Survivor | **TOVA FRIEDMAN**

I have always loved tzimmes. My late husband's favorite food was tzimmes, but he also shared his family's recipe for kasha varnishkes. So from the time I had my own family and had children, we always used to prepare tzimmes and varnishkes.

This is the "old-fashioned" way to make it: with lots of mushrooms.

SERVES 4 AS A MAIN DISH, 6–8 AS A SIDE DISH

4 cups water
1 cup kasha (buckwheat groats)
1 extra-large egg, beaten
Salt
1 cup bowtie (farfalle) pasta
3 tablespoons butter or vegetable oil
1 large yellow onion, diced
12 ounces white mushrooms, sliced about ¼ inch thick
3 cloves garlic, minced
¼ cup soy sauce

Note: Bowties are added last to keep them white.

Bring 4 cups of water to a boil and have it ready. Put the kasha in a medium bowl. Add the beaten egg to the dry kasha. Mix thoroughly so all the grains are uniformly coated.

Heat a heavy-bottom 8-quart pot over medium-high heat until it is very hot. Add the kasha-egg mixture and stir continuously, breaking up clumps so that the kasha is very hot. Slowly pour the boiling water onto the hot kasha and add a pinch of salt. The kasha will explode and froth (this is the fun part). After all the water has been added and the pot settles down, skim any schmutz that might be floating on top. Reduce the heat to low, cover, and cook until the water is absorbed, about 30 minutes.

While the kasha is cooking, prepare the bowtie pasta according to package instructions (cook in salted water for about 12 minutes).

While bowties are cooking, heat the butter (or oil, if parve) in a wide saucepan. Add the onion and cook until slightly softened, about 5 minutes. Add the mushrooms and then the garlic and cook until the mushrooms and onions are tender. Add the cooked kasha to the mushroom mixture, then add the soy sauce and toss gently to coat. Add the bowties just before serving.

An alternative way of cooking this dish is to place the kasha mixture in a casserole dish and bake at 300°F for 20 minutes, or to desired dryness. When ready to serve, add bowties and mix. Serve hot.

COOKIES *and* TREATS

עוגיות ומתוקים

JELLY COOKIES

Survivor | **LOIS FLAMHOLZ**

This recipe has a secret ingredient: a thimble. Lois's son recalls that when he tried to recreate the recipe, the cookies never turned out quite as good as hers: "The problem was, I never had a thimble." "You can't just use any thimble," Lois says. "It's gotta be the special thimble that has the hole on the bottom—you know, the one that real tailors use, that's open on both ends. The bottom end is a little bit sharper, so that's how you cut the cookies."

YIELDS ABOUT 100 COOKIES

- 5 cups all-purpose flour
- 1 cup (2 sticks) margarine, softened, plus more for greasing the pans
- ½ cup (1 stick) butter, softened
- 2 eggs, separated, whites beaten
- 2 teaspoons vanilla extract
- 1 cup vanilla yogurt
- Apricot jam, for filling
- ½ cup sugar, for sprinkling

In a large bowl, mix the flour, margarine, butter, egg yolks, vanilla, and yogurt. Knead the dough until it comes away clean from your hands. Wrap and refrigerate overnight.

When ready to assemble, preheat the oven to 350°F and lightly grease two cookie sheets.

Roll out the dough thin and cut out into small circles. Make a hole in the middle of half of the circles using a thimble or the smallest cookie cutter you have. On the uncut circles, spread a small amount of apricot jam and cover with the cut circles. Press down the edges, then dip in beaten egg white. Sprinkle the tops with sugar.

Working in batches, place the cookies on two or more cookie sheets and bake until light brown, about 40 minutes.

BLUEBERRY STONEKES

Survivor | **DAVID LENGA**

I was eleven years old when the war broke out. I was very eager to help my mom: washing the dishes, peeling potatoes, or helping with whatever she needed me to do in the kitchen—and she was grateful for that. I noticed how diligently she worked to put the ingredients together for the blueberry stonekes. The end product was so delicious—better than any bakery could possibly bake. The whole family was wild about them. When you bit into the stonekes, they were full of blueberries and sugar—so juicy—the taste has stayed with me forever. The stonekes remained so much in my memory that I taught my wife how to make them when I got married.

YIELDS 10 PASTRIES

FOR THE BLUEBERRY FILLING:

3 cups blueberries, plus a few reserved berries for each pastry
1 cup sugar
2 heaping tablespoons cornstarch

FOR THE PASTRY:

1½ cups all-purpose flour, plus more for rolling
Pinch of salt
4 tablespoons sugar
1 cup (2 sticks) cold butter, cut in small cubes
2 large egg yolks
1 teaspoon vanilla extract
¼ cup ice water

FOR THE EGG WASH:

1 large egg
1 teaspoon cold water

Make the filling: In a medium saucepan, bring the berries and sugar to a gentle boil over medium heat and continue to simmer for about 15 minutes. (Some juice should steam off, which concentrates the blueberry flavor.) Mix the cornstarch with about ¼ cup water and slowly pour it into the boiling berries, stirring constantly. Continue to stir and boil gently for 1 more minute. Remove from the heat and allow to cool to room temperature, stirring occasionally. Chill completely in the refrigerator.

Make the pastry: In a large bowl, mix the flour, salt, and sugar. Add the butter to the dry ingredients and mix until it looks like coarse meal with pea-size pieces of butter remaining in the mixture.

In a separate bowl, whisk together the egg yolks, vanilla, and ice water and pour the mixture over the dry ingredients. Mix gently with a wooden spoon until a soft dough forms (or use a food processor). Divide the dough into 2 disks, then wrap in plastic wrap and let rest in the refrigerator for 20 minutes.

On a floured surface, roll each portion of the dough out to about ⅛ inch thick, or roughly a 10-by-15-inch rectangle. (The dough will be sticky, so use a lot of flour on the board and rolling pin.) Cut the dough into 5-inch rounds, using a cutter or an object with a similar diameter, like a large empty can or a plastic container. Lay the rounds out on floured cookie sheets.

For the egg wash: Whisk egg and 1 teaspoon cold water together in a small bowl. Brush the edges of each round with the egg wash, then scoop heaping tablespoons of the blueberry compote into the centers. Add a few whole berries to each one to give it more juiciness. Fold the dough over from both sides to form a long, oval-shaped pastry. Pinch the top closed, then brush with more egg wash. Cut 3 small slits in the center of each one with a sharp knife to allow the steam to vent.

Before baking, chill the pastries in the refrigerator for 20 minutes and preheat the oven to 400°F. Bake the pastries for 10 minutes, then reduce the heat to 375°F and cook for an additional 15 minutes, or until the tops are evenly golden brown. Carefully remove to a wire rack to cool.

WALNUT COOKIES

Survivor | **GOLDIE FINKELSTEIN**

Goldie's son Joe recalls: My mother was very proprietary with her recipes. We asked her many times what the recipe was, and she would say, "Never mind; it's too hard. You won't be able to do it. I'll do it for you." Once we got the recipes, we found out that that was actually true. They were very hard. You don't make a gourmet offering without effort. But I think it was not only that she was protecting us from working too hard. I think if she gave it away, she wouldn't still have it to give. She wanted to keep giving it. She didn't want to give it away. It was all about the process of sharing.

YIELDS 60 COOKIES

FOR THE DOUGH:

½ pound butter, softened
3 ounces cream cheese, softened
1 cup brown sugar
½ teaspoon vanilla extract
2½ cups all-purpose flour, plus more as needed
3½ teaspoons baking powder

FOR THE TOPPING:

¾ cup chopped walnuts
6 heaping tablespoons sugar
2 eggs (can use egg whites only, if preferred)

Make the dough: In a large bowl using an electric mixer, cream the butter, cream cheese, and brown sugar. Mix in the vanilla. In a separate bowl, whisk together the flour and baking powder. Mix the flour into the wet ingredients until a dough forms. Add more flour if the dough feels too wet. On a floured work surface, roll the dough into cylinders, 1 to 1½ inches in diameter. Wrap in wax paper and refrigerate for a few hours or overnight.

Preheat oven to 350°F and set an oven rack to the top position. Line cookie sheets with wax paper.

Make the topping: Combine the walnuts and sugar in a small bowl. In a separate bowl, beat the egg (or egg whites only, if preferred).

Cut the dough into ¼-inch slices. Dip each slice into the egg, then into the sugar-nut mixture. Place 1 to 2 inches apart on the cookie sheets and bake for 10 minutes on the top oven rack, until lightly golden.

CAPPUCCINO COOKIES

Survivor | **RUTH WEBBER**

YIELDS 72 COOKIES

2 squares (1 ounce) unsweetened chocolate
½ cup (1 stick) margarine or butter, room temperature, plus more for greasing
½ cup plus 3 tablespoons vegetable shortening
½ cup granulated sugar
½ cup packed brown sugar
1 tablespoon instant coffee
1 teaspoon hot water
1 large egg
2 cups all-purpose flour
1 teaspoon ground cinnamon
¼ teaspoon salt
1½ cups semisweet chocolate chips

Melt the unsweetened chocolate in the microwave on medium heat or in a saucepan over low heat. Set aside to cool slightly.

In a large bowl, use an electric mixer to beat the margarine and ½ cup shortening until smooth. Add both sugars and beat until fluffy. Dissolve the coffee in hot water and add to the margarine mixture along with the melted chocolate and the egg. Beat well.

In a separate bowl, mix the flour, cinnamon, and salt. Use a wooden spoon to beat the dry ingredients into the margarine mixture. Cover and chill for 1 hour, or until the dough is firm enough to handle. Shape into two 2-inch-diameter logs, wrap in plastic wrap, and refrigerate overnight.

When ready, preheat the oven to 350°F and lightly grease several cookie sheets.

Cut the dough into ¼-inch slices and place on cookie sheets, spacing the slices about 2 inches apart. Bake for 10 to 12 minutes, until set and lightly golden. Let cool while you repeat with the remaining dough.

Meanwhile, prepare the coating. Melt the chocolate chips with the remaining 3 tablespoons shortening in the microwave or in a small saucepan set over low heat, stirring to combine.

Once all the cookies are completely cool, dip half of each cookie in the chocolate-shortening mixture and place them on cold, wax paper–lined cookie sheets. Refrigerate or freeze until the chocolate is hard. Remove promptly and serve, or store in an airtight container in the refrigerator or freezer until ready to serve.

HAMANTASCHEN

(Yiddish: homentashn)

Survivors | **IRENE BUCHMAN AND OLGA JAEGER**

Irene's daughter Carol remembers: As Irene and Olga's children, we always knew the upcoming Jewish holidays based on the ingredients found in the refrigerator and pantry. If we saw apricot jam, prune lekvar, and mohn (ground poppy seeds), we knew Purim was around the corner. The sisters would schlep us kids to the fishmongers in Washington Heights, looking for the freshest whitefish and carp, which was our clue that it was either Rosh Hashanah or Pesach. If there was farmer cheese, cream cheese, and pot cheese, get ready for the blintzes and cheese Danish contest. We didn't need the four seasons or a calendar to know what was coming next, food was our guide.

These triangle-shaped, sweet-filled cookies are typically prepared to celebrate Purim, a festival holiday. While my mom made the hamantaschen with cookie dough, my aunt Olga made them with challah. I have always preferred my mom's recipe. It has just the right texture. My mom's preferred hamantaschen filling was always the apricot jam. She would not put too much of it in, just the right amount. Also, her secret tip was always to pinch the sides while forming the treats.

My mother, Irene, taught me at a young age to drink tea and coffee without sugar. One of my favorite memories is eating hamantaschen and drinking black coffee with them. I loved the contrast between the sweetness of the treat and the bitterness of the hot drink. I have savored every moment of this particular memory I share with my mom.

YIELDS 30–40 COOKIES

1 cup sugar
½ cup vegetable oil
⅓ cup vegetable shortening, plus more for greasing the pans
3 eggs
½ cup orange juice
4 cups all-purpose flour, plus more for rolling
3 teaspoons baking powder
1 teaspoon salt
Jam of choice, for filling (optional: nuts, chocolate)

Preheat the oven to 350°F and grease two baking sheets.

In a large bowl, cream the sugar, oil, and shortening. Add the eggs and orange juice and mix well.

In a separate bowl, whisk together the flour, baking powder, and salt. Add to the sugar mixture and mix until a crumbly dough forms.

Knead the dough with your hands until it becomes a smooth ball. Divide the dough in half. Lightly flour a work surface. Working with half of the dough at a time, use a rolling pin to roll each portion ¼ inch thick. Cut out circles from the dough with a 3-inch cookie cutter or rim of a drinking glass. Drop 1 teaspoon of jam (you can add nuts and chocolate) into the middle of each circle (my mother used apricot or prune jam). Take the left side of the circle and fold it toward the center to cover the left third of the circle. Now take the right side of the circle and fold it toward the center to create a triangular tip at the top. Finally, take the bottom part of the circle and fold it upward to complete the triangle. Pinch all three corners to secure them. Repeat with the rest of the dough and jam to make the remaining cookies, placing them on the prepared baking sheets as they are made.

Bake for about 20 minutes, until the cookies are golden brown in color.

MANDELBROT

Survivor | **RUTH WEBBER**

Mandelbrot, literally translated as "almond bread," also known as mandel bread, is a sweet, almond-flavored cookie. My family would eat mandelbrot all the time. This recipe was not reserved for holidays or special occasions. I would bake them as often as possible because everyone enjoyed them. Even our family in Israel learned to love them when they would visit—and I have taken a few batches with me on trips there.

I used to make these with a special kind of bitter almond—now unavailable. So now I use a regular almond, which is still good—but the bitter almond added an exceptional taste.

YIELDS ABOUT 30 COOKIES

3½ cups all-purpose flour, plus more for kneading
2 teaspoons baking powder
½ cup slivered almonds
3 eggs
¾ cup sugar
¾ cup vegetable oil
1 teaspoon vanilla extract
½ teaspoon almond extract

Preheat the oven to 350°F. Line two baking sheets or cookie sheets with parchment paper.

In a medium bowl, mix the flour and baking powder together. Stir in the almonds and set aside.

In the bowl of an electric mixer, beat the eggs until thick and very light. With the mixer continuing to beat, gradually add the sugar. When well combined, slowly pour in the oil while beating. When well combined, add the vanilla and almond extracts. With the mixer on low speed, incorporate the dry ingredients, about a third at a time, mixing well.

Knead the dough on a floured board for 10 to 12 turns, then divide the dough into 3 or 4 pieces. Roll each piece into strips about 3 inches wide, 1 inch thick, and 10 inches long (or a length that will comfortably fit your pan).

Place each piece on the prepared pan and bake for 35 minutes, or until golden brown. Remove immediately to a cutting board. While still warm, carefully cut into ½-inch slices. Lay the slices on their sides on the baking sheet and return to the oven to brown delicately, 5 to 10 minutes. Remove from the oven and let cool completely.

GOLDIE'S RUGELACH

Survivor | **GOLDIE FINKELSTEIN**

Goldie's son Joe recalls: My mother was eleven years old when the war started. As she grew up in a very wealthy family with live-in servants, a live-in maid, and a live-in cook, she did not know anything about cooking. Her mother worked in the family business, so it wasn't like she spent a lot of time in the kitchen with her mother making pancakes and cookies. It didn't happen. She was a very sheltered, pampered rich girl. She was taken to camp when she was thirteen and liberated when she was fifteen. So, she missed her whole adolescence, and she was the sole survivor of her family.

My father once said to me, "When your mother married me, she didn't know how to boil water. She couldn't even cook an egg. She didn't know anything." She made it a goal in life to become an Iron Chef. She became a fabulous cook. Not just because she learned from other people, but she took it to the next level. All the recipes in this cookbook are her originals. She learned, she cooked, and she experimented. That's all she did after World War II. I think her best recipe was rugelach. If anything was gold, they were titanium. I've never had, before or after, rugelach that tasted like that.

YIELDS ABOUT 100 RUGELACH

FOR THE DOUGH:

¼-ounce envelope active dry yeast
¼ cup warm water
1 pound cream cheese (2 blocks), softened
1 pound (4 sticks) butter, softened
4¼ cups all-purpose flour

Make the dough: Dissolve the yeast in the warm water and let sit until slightly foamy.

In a large bowl, mix the cream cheese and butter until smooth. Pour in the proofed yeast, then slowly add the flour, mixing well with your hands to work the dough to the proper consistency: a little sticky and flaky. Divide the dough into 4 or 5 balls. Wrap each in wax paper and refrigerate overnight.

When ready to assemble, preheat the oven to 350°F and coat several cookie sheets with nonstick cooking spray. Allow the refrigerated dough to rest at room temperature before using.

FOR THE FILLING:

½–¾ cup walnuts

2 tablespoons butter, melted

1 cup granulated sugar, plus more for dusting

1 teaspoon vanilla extract

2 tablespoons milk

½ cup packed raisins

½ teaspoon ground cinnamon

FOR FINISHING:

Confectioners' sugar

Vanilla sugar

Make the filling: Grind the walnuts very finely in a blender or food processor. Add the butter and mix it into the walnuts. Add the granulated sugar, vanilla, milk, raisins, and cinnamon and blend to form a paste.

Make the rugelach: Spread confectioners' sugar on your work surface (not flour). Roll out each dough ball into a 16- to 19-inch-diameter disk and cut each disk through the center into 20 to 24 wedges. Place some filling on each wedge near the wider end, or top. Roll each wedge down from the top into a crescent. Flatten the crescent a little and pinch the ends a bit to seal the sides closed, so the filling does not flow out.

Place the crescents on the prepared cookie sheets. Dust the crescents with granulated sugar. Working in batches as needed, bake for 20 to 22 minutes, until light golden brown. Let cool before removing the rugelach from the cookie sheet.

When ready to serve, sprinkle with a 50/50 mix of confectioners' sugar and vanilla sugar.

Notes: This recipe is not parve.

APPLE COBBLER

Survivor | **RUTH WEBBER**

Since this recipe calls for cornstarch, which some families omit during Passover, I recommend substituting it with potato starch or arrowroot or getting kosher cornstarch.

SERVES 12–16

FOR THE TOPPING:

1½ cups granulated sugar
1 cup parve margarine, cut into thin slices, at room temperature
⅔ cup vegetable shortening
2½ ounces almond paste, crumbled
2 cups all-purpose flour
1 teaspoon pure almond extract

FOR THE FILLING:

4 tablespoons fresh lemon juice
5 pounds Golden Delicious apples
⅔ cup packed light brown sugar
½ cup granulated sugar
3 tablespoons cornstarch
1 teaspoon ground cinnamon
½ teaspoon freshly grated nutmeg
1½ cups raisins, soaked in warm water for 20 minutes and drained
2 tablespoons brandy
1 teaspoon vanilla extract

Make the topping: In a stand mixer using the paddle attachment, beat together the sugar, margarine, shortening, and almond paste until smooth. Add the flour and almond extract and mix just until combined. Form into a thick disk, and wrap in plastic wrap. Refrigerate until well chilled, about 4 hours or overnight.

Preheat the oven to 425°F and grease a 9-by-13-inch baking dish with nonstick cooking spray or shortening.

Make the filling: Stir 2 tablespoons of the lemon juice in a large bowl of cold water, enough to cover the apples after they are prepared. Peel, core, and cut each apple into ½-inch-thick wedges. Drop the cut wedges into the lemon water. Set aside.

In another large bowl, mix the brown and granulated sugars, cornstarch, cinnamon, and nutmeg. Drain the apples well and add them to the sugar mixture, tossing to coat. Add the raisins and sprinkle with the remaining 2 tablespoons lemon juice. Stir in the brandy and vanilla. Transfer to the prepared baking dish and spread into an even layer.

Remove the prepared topping from the refrigerator and use the large holes on a box grater to grate the topping all over the filling, letting it fall randomly. Do not pack, or the topping will not be delicately crunchy when baked. Bake on the middle rack until the topping is crisp and golden brown and the apples are tender, about 1 hour. Cool slightly, then serve warm.

BIRD'S MILK

(Hungarian: madártej)

Survivor | **ANGELA OROSZ-RICHT**

When I was a kid, I was a very picky eater. My mother had a hard time finding dishes that I would eat. This recipe was one of the things I loved, so every week, she would make this for me as a dessert.

She usually served it on Sundays in individual teacups or ramekins. I have a very vivid memory of my mother serving our meals on her gorgeous dining set. She loved beautiful objects and chose to celebrate every day, not just the holidays or Shabbat, by eating off lovely plates and cups. I still remember that the cups had a small grape pattern.

What makes this recipe particularly delicious is the combination of the vanilla and whipped eggs: the flavor and the texture. On rare occasions when my mother bought raisins, we would add raisins to this dessert.

SERVES 6–8

3 tablespoons vanilla extract (or 1 vanilla pod)
4 cups whole milk
6 eggs, separated
6 tablespoons sugar
Lemon zest (optional)

If using, slice the top outer layer of the vanilla pod in half lengthwise and use a spoon to scrape out the seeds inside. Heat the milk in a large pot over medium heat. Add vanilla seeds or extract and heat until hot but not boiling.

In a large bowl, beat the egg whites with an electric mixer until stiff peaks form. When the milk is hot, use a spoon to form the egg whites into dollops and place them into the pan. Cook on one side for about 2 minutes, then flip, cover the pot, and cook for another 2 minutes. Remove the dollops from the milk and place them in a strainer or colander.

In a medium bowl, beat the egg yolks with the sugar until thick and light yellow. Add the egg-yolk mixture to the hot milk and stir continuously. To prevent the eggs from scrambling, do not let the mixture boil. Keep stirring until creamy, then remove from heat and continue to stir for another minute.

Pour the custard into nice serving bowls and leave to cool. To serve, place the cooked egg-white dollops on top of the custard and sprinkle with lemon zest (if using).

CINNAMON SNOWBALLS

Survivor | **RUTH WEBBER**

(submitted in memory of her Aunt Freida)

Frieda was my husband's aunt, and she was a surrogate grandmother to my children since she did not have children of her own. She made these cinnamon snowballs often. It seemed she always had them at hand when we came over, and especially for every holiday event. Aunt Frieda used to invite the whole family for Passover and Rosh Hashanah. It was not until she became older that I took over as the main chef and host of the family holiday gatherings.

YIELDS ABOUT 18 COOKIES

- 1 cup (2 sticks) margarine, softened
- ½ cup plus scant ¼ cup sugar
- ½ teaspoon vanilla extract
- 1¾ cups all-purpose flour, sifted
- 1¼ teaspoons ground cinnamon

Cream the margarine in a large bowl. Gradually add ½ cup sugar and beat until light and fluffy. Mix in the vanilla. Add the flour and 1 teaspoon of the cinnamon and mix until incorporated. Cover the bowl and chill the dough in the refrigerator for several hours.

When ready to bake, preheat the oven to 350°F. Use teaspoons to shape the chilled dough into 1-inch balls and place them on an ungreased cookie sheet with equal space between them. Bake on the middle rack for 15 minutes, or until lightly golden, watching carefully to make sure they don't get too dark.

Remove the cookie sheet to a wire rack. Stir together the scant ¼ cup sugar and remaining ¼ teaspoon cinnamon and sprinkle the topping over the cookies while they're still hot from the oven. Serve.

KOGEL MOGEL

(Yiddish: gogl-mogl)

Survivor | **EUGENE GINTER**

After the war, I was emaciated and not interested in food. Food would make me sick. My mother would make me certain foods that I could stomach to fatten me up, like this sweet, calorie-heavy kogel mogel. I was delighted when my mother made this dish for me. I remember her using an old-fashioned handheld mixer. It was easy to make and had a very sweet taste. You could doctor it up by mixing cocoa powder in it, or you could pour cognac or whiskey into it. Use enough sugar for your taste. I loved having it on various occasions.

SERVES 1

2 or 3 eggs, separated
Sugar

Beat egg whites to a firm state with an electric mixer. Add yolks and sugar. Beat until smooth.

Notes: Vanilla extract or powdered cocoa can be added for flavor. This recipe uses uncooked eggs; alternatively you can use pasteurized eggs that come in a pourable carton.

Cogel Mogel

2 or 3 Eggs, seperated.
Sugar

Beat eggs whites to a firm state with electric mixer.
Add yolk and sugar
Beat until smooth.

CHEESECAKE MILKSHAKE

Survivor | **DAVID MARKS**

My wife, Kathy, and I love buttermilk but realize many people do not. But who doesn't love cheesecake? My grandmother would make a special treat as a child, calling it a "cheesecake milkshake." I think she discovered it by accident, a mistake. Later I found out the two simple ingredients, transforming one of the ingredients that I love but some people find revolting, into a delicious treat.

We drink it now as an occasional refreshing summer treat. We love serving it to others, calling it a "cheesecake milkshake," to the raves and ahhs as they sip, and then watching their shocked expression of amazement when they find out the two simple ingredients, especially the buttermilk. It is a fun and easy treat.

SERVES 1–2

Several scoops of vanilla ice cream
Approximately an equal amount of buttermilk

Put the ice cream and buttermilk in a blender. Process until smooth. Pour into a glass and serve.

CAKES

עוגות

PLUM CAKE

(German: Pflaumenkuchen)

Survivor | **CLAIRE HEYMANN**

Claire's daughter Helen recalls: My maternal grandfather went to Dachau early on, 1938 or 1939, when it was strictly a work camp. But he came back, and although he was an insurance broker, he learned how to be a baker to have a trade when he came to America. My mom's parents had applied for their number to get out of the country and get to the United States, but it never actually happened. However, thanks to my mother's father's baking practice, this Pflaumenkuchen became a staple recipe in my mother's life. It was one of the cakes her father learned to bake in anticipation of coming to America and working as a baker.

This is a very traditional German cake. If it's served with whipped cream on top, it evokes memories of the sophisticated big-city life, like Cologne. If it's served without whipped cream, it's more of a country recipe. I have many memories of this cake being served at home whenever friends would come over. It was always everyone's favorite.

It's important to note that only Italian plums work for this type of cake. They are only in season in late summer and early fall.

SERVES 12

1½ pounds Italian plums, pitted and sliced
9 tablespoons butter, softened
8½ tablespoons granulated sugar
1½ teaspoons vanilla sugar, or 1–2 teaspoons vanilla extract
2 eggs
1¾ cups all-purpose flour
1 teaspoon baking powder

Preheat the oven to 350°F and grease the bottom of an 11-inch springform pan.

Beat the butter with 6 tablespoons of the granulated sugar and the vanilla sugar or extract until smooth and creamy. Stir in the eggs one by one. Mix the flour with the baking powder and gradually stir in until light and foamy.

Pour the batter into the pan and spread to coat the bottom. Arrange the plums on top, cut side up. Bake for about 50 minutes, until the top is browned and the plums have softened. Remove from the oven, sprinkle with the remaining 2½ tablespoons granulated sugar, and allow to cool in the pan before serving.

Note: A jelly-roll pan can work as well and yields a cake that is relatively easy to cut and serve.

CHEESECAKE

Survivor | **RUTH WEBBER**

(submitted in memory of Malka "Molly" Muschkies, her mother)

I would always make this cheesecake in a regular 9-by-13 pan. I always cool the cheesecake completely, then cut it into squares and serve as individual pieces.

You will know that the cheesecake is cooked, done, and set when you shake the pan and see how much it "jiggles." It shouldn't move too much when it is ready to come out. Also, it should be very slightly brown on top.

SERVES 10–15

- 1½ cups graham cracker crumbs (from about 10 full sheets of crackers)
- 6 tablespoons unsalted butter, melted
- 2 tablespoons brown sugar
- 4 eggs
- 1 tablespoon vanilla extract, plus more for the sour cream layer
- 1 cup plus 3 tablespoons granulated sugar
- 1½ pounds (three 8-ounce blocks) cream cheese, softened
- Ground cinnamon, for sprinkling
- 2 cups sour cream

Preheat the oven to 375°F.

In a large bowl, mix the graham cracker crumbs, melted butter, and brown sugar. Press into the bottom of a 9-inch round springform pan.

Mix the eggs, 1 tablespoon vanilla, 1 cup granulated sugar, and cream cheese until smooth. Pour the filling over the crust. Bake for 30 minutes, then remove the pan from the oven and sprinkle with cinnamon. Stir together the sour cream, remaining 3 tablespoons granulated sugar, and vanilla to taste and spread over the cinnamon. Bake for an additional 15 minutes, or until the cheesecake is nearly set. Remove from the oven and let cool completely. Chill and serve.

FRUIT TART

(German: Tortenboden)

Survivor | **ANNELIESE NOSSBAUM**

Anneliese's children, Jeffrey, Jan, and Eileen, recall: The Tortenboden was a real treat. It was the tart that Mom would make for birthdays and special occasions. We particularly remember it being served as dessert, along with fragrant coffee, during visits with dear friends who were also German Jews who lived in New York. Mom would bring out her delicate china and her beautiful cloth tablecloth and napkins. Everything looked elegant, and I would imagine we were in Europe. We would sit around the dining room table for hours. The room was filled with the warmth of good friends, sparkling with love, laughter, and good conversation. We loved these visits, and these friends were the closest to a family that we had.

There were always canned peaches lined up in concentric circles in Anneliese's kitchen. If it was berry season, Anneliese put berries in to cover the spaces between the peach slices. Raspberries were her favorite by far! Occasionally there was a banana sliced on there as well. The "glaze" she put on the top went on fresh fruit as well as canned fruit. It made it shiny and sticky and extra sweet!

The Tortenboden started with a crispy shell, but Anneliese let it soak in the fruit juices and glazes overnight so that the crust was soft and gooey on top and crisp underneath. She would always give everyone a small slice to start with, but everyone helped themselves to seconds and thirds until the whole tart was gone, never a leftover!

YIELDS 1 TART, PLUS 2 ADDITIONAL CRUSTS

FOR THE DOUGH (YIELDS 3 CRUSTS):

½ cup (1 stick) butter, softened, plus more for greasing pans
1½ cups sugar, or less, to taste

Preheat the oven to 350°F and grease the bottoms and sides of three tart pans or glass pie plates.

Make the dough: Mix the butter, sugar, and eggs in a large bowl. Add the flour and mix, followed by the whiskey (if using). Mix in the baking soda last, then form into a dough and divide into 3 equal parts.

Shape the dough into disks and press the dough into the bottom and sides of the pans. Bake for 15 to 20 minutes, or

3 large eggs (or 2 if using extra large)
2½ cups all-purpose flour
1 tablespoon whiskey (optional)
1½ teaspoons baking soda

FOR THE TOPPING (FOR 1 TART):

29-ounce can whole peaches (or halved apricots) in heavy syrup (reserve the syrup and halve the peaches), or an equivalent quantity of sliced fresh fruits (such as bananas, blueberries, strawberries) tossed with ½ cup sugar to macerate
1 heaping teaspoon cornstarch
2–3 teaspoons fresh lemon or orange juice

until golden brown. Set aside to cool. (The extra crusts can be frozen at this point and saved for later.)

Top the tart: Spread all but ¼ cup of the reserved fruit syrup evenly onto the prepared crust. Place the peaches or apricots decoratively on top.

Pour the remaining ¼ cup fruit syrup into a small saucepan. Add the cornstarch and lemon or orange juice. Bring to a boil, stir to dissolve the cornstarch, then pour over the fruit to cover. Leave to cool slightly, then wrap and chill in the refrigerator, preferably overnight. Serve cold.

GRANDMA'S APPLE CAKE

Survivor | **GOLDIE FINKELSTEIN**

Goldie's son Joe recalls: Everyone in our family would bug my mother constantly for the recipes, and she would put them off. My sister-in-law, Gail, finally said to my mother: "Could I watch you? Can I follow you and see what you're doing, and you can explain it to me?" My mother said, "Yeah, OK." She would follow her around the kitchen on holidays and say, "What are you doing? How much are you putting in?" My mother would say a handful of this and half a handful of that, a pinch of this or a little bit of that. Gail would try to see what my mother was putting in, and then she would take the same ingredient and try to measure it and take notes. Then she would go home afterward and try to replicate it as a scientist would do. Very often, she found that it failed. It was not like anything my mother did. At first, we thought she was leaving out ingredients. What my sister-in-law did took years to accomplish. She would watch and measure and experiment. It would fail, and she would go back repeatedly until the recipe was at least similar to what my mother made, so we could feel like we had the recipe. She did say to my mother, "Who's going to remember this when you're not here?" So finally, toward the end, my mother was a little bit more forthcoming. But the recipes here are not what my mother said at all. They are what Gail observed my mother doing, or information she got when she asked her questions, and then trial and error until she got it right and it worked the way my mother described it. It was a labor of love.

SERVES 10

FOR THE DOUGH:

- 3½–4 cups all-purpose flour
- 1 egg
- 2 egg yolks
- 1 cup sugar
- 1 cup sour cream
- 1 cup (2 sticks) cold margarine, cut into pieces
- 1 teaspoon vanilla extract

Prepare the dough: Using your hands, mix 3 cups of the flour with the whole egg, the 2 egg yolks, sugar, sour cream, margarine, and vanilla. Mix in enough of the additional flour (up to 1 cup more) to form a dough. Roll into a ball, divide in half, and shape into two disks. Wrap in plastic wrap and refrigerate for at least several hours, or overnight.

Prepare the filling: Put the apples in a medium bowl and toss with a little flour to absorb extra moisture. Add sugar and lemon juice to taste. Stir in the raisins.

FOR THE FILLING AND ASSEMBLY:

3 pounds apples, sliced or grated into large pieces
Up to ½ cup all-purpose flour
Sugar, to taste
Lemon juice, to taste
½ cup raisins, or more to taste
2–3 egg yolks, for brushing the dough
½ cup marmalade
½ teaspoon ground cinnamon, or to taste

Preheat the oven to 350°F and grease a 9-by-13-inch cake pan or a deep-dish pie pan.

Assemble the cake: On a lightly floured work surface, roll half the dough out to form a rectangle large enough to cover the bottom and sides of the pan. Press the dough into the pan and brush with egg yolk. Roll out the other piece of dough into a 9-by-13-inch rectangle.

Strain the apples and fill the pan with them. Dot with the marmalade and sprinkle with cinnamon to taste.

Cover the apple filling with the remaining sheet of dough, pinching the edges to seal. Brush with more egg yolk and run a fork through the yolk to create a design, then cut slits in the top. Sprinkle the top with sugar.

Bake for 30 to 45 minutes, or until golden brown.

Note: One pound apples equals 3 medium apples, which equals 3 cups of sliced apples.

APPLE CAKE

Survivor | **LOIS FLAMHOLZ**

I learned to bake this cake from my mother. After the war, when I moved to the United States, I was a life member of Hadassah. I was on the board for years, and the board meetings were always at somebody's house. Sometimes we would only have four or five people come to the board meetings. When it was at my house, the whole board came because they knew I would serve my delicious apple cake. And once a year, we'd have a bazaar for Hadassah to raise money, and everybody had to bring something. I baked the apple cake, and they used to fight over it. There were a couple of people who would cut it in half. That way, the cake could be enjoyed by two separate buyers.

SERVES 12

FOR THE DOUGH:

- ¾ cup (1½ sticks) margarine, plus more for greasing the pan
- 2 cups all-purpose flour
- 2 teaspoons baking powder
- 4 eggs
- 1 cup sugar

FOR THE FILLING:

- Apricot jam
- At least 4 apples, preferably Cortland or Granny Smith
- Ground cinnamon, to taste
- ½ cup sugar
- Juice of ½ lemon
- 1 egg, beaten (optional)

Preheat the oven to 350°F and grease an 8-by-14-inch baking pan with margarine.

Make the dough: Mix the flour, baking powder, ¾ cup margarine, eggs, and sugar to form a dough. Divide in half and roll out half the dough onto the greased pan.

Make the filling: Spread apricot jam on the dough.

Peel the apples, cut into quarters and then cut the quarters into slices. Spread the apples very thickly over the dough. Sprinkle cinnamon and a little sugar on the apples and squeeze the juice of the half lemon over the apples. Thinly roll out the other half of the dough and use it to top the apples.

If you like, brush the egg on top to create a shiny glaze. Bake the cake for about 1 hour, but check earlier to see if it starts to brown on top.

Note: Lois prefers to make her own dough, but store-bought is also fine in a pinch!

SPONGE CAKE

Survivor | **MIRIAM ZIEGLER**
(submitted in memory of her bubbe, Fanny, and her mother, Rosie)

When I came to Canada, I came first as an orphan because my mother couldn't come. She arrived a year later with my aunt and my grandmother. The three of them started cooking. They couldn't afford to go to a restaurant at that time or anything. We lived in an attic, but we could use the kitchen, and they started baking. This sponge cake recipe is theirs. It was passed down to me by my mother. I always bake it in my mother's old sponge cake pans. The pans are now 70-plus-years-old aluminum tube pans. I believe the pans give the cake its exceptional taste. What makes this cake delicious is the fluffy texture and not-too-sweet flavor.

One of my favorite memories connected to this recipe is quite charming. I was invited to a friend's party and decided to bake this sponge cake in advance. When I arrived at the party, I realized it was a surprise twenty-fifth wedding anniversary party for my husband, Roman, and me organized by our three children. I looked at the sweet table and saw my cake on the table. I cherish that memory.

SERVES 16–24

10 large eggs, separated
1 teaspoon cream of tartar
1¼ cups sugar, plus 1 tablespoon for sprinkling on top
Zest and juice of 1 small orange
Zest and juice of 1 small lemon
1 cup all-purpose flour
2 teaspoons baking powder
1 teaspoon vanilla extract
2 teaspoons almond extract

Preheat the oven to 350°F and lightly grease a 10-inch tube pan. In the bowl of an electric mixer, beat the egg whites with the cream of tartar on high until stiff peaks form.

In a clean mixer bowl on low speed, beat the egg yolks, ½ cup sugar, and orange and lemon zest and juices. Slowly add flour, baking powder, vanilla and almond extracts, and remaining ¾ cup sugar and mix until well combined. Gently fold the egg whites into the yolk mixture, a third at a time.

Pour batter into the prepared pan. Sprinkle 1 tablespoon sugar on top of the cake for a crustier top. Bake on the middle rack for 1 hour, or until a toothpick inserted in the center comes out clean. Cool upside down on a rack.

When cool, take a thin spatula and loosen the sides of the cake; turn over and carefully lift the pan off. Then take a knife and slide it along the top of the cake; the middle of the tube pan should lift off easily.

SARAH'S FAMOUS SPONGE CAKE

(Yiddish: leykech)

Survivor | **DAVID LENGA**

My mother was very famous for her leykech (Yiddish for sponge cake). My mom really knew how to prepare this dessert. The fantastic thing is that my wife was born in Czechoslovakia, where the Jewish cuisine resembles the Jewish cuisine in Poland (where I am from). The funny thing is that my wife—a pretty young girl herself during the wartime—learned from her mother and grandmother before the war started. After the war, she created a sponge cake that was unlike anything her friends could come close to, becoming very famous for that.

SERVES 12–24

- ½ cup vegetable oil, plus more for the pan
- 1½ cups all-purpose flour, plus more for the pan
- 9 eggs, separated
- 1½ cups sugar
- ½ cup orange juice
- ½ cup cold water
- 2 teaspoons baking powder
- 1 tablespoon cocoa powder

Preheat the oven to 275°F and oil and flour an angel food cake pan.

In the bowl of an electric mixer, beat the egg whites with ¾ cup sugar until stiff peaks form. Set aside.

In a separate bowl, mix the egg yolks, remaining ¾ cup sugar, ½ cup oil, orange juice, and cold water. In another bowl, whisk together 1½ cups flour, baking powder, and cocoa powder, then slowly stir the dry ingredients into the yolk mixture until well blended. Gently fold in the egg whites.

Pour the batter into the prepared pan and carefully place it in the preheated oven. Bake for 10 minutes. Increase the temperature to 350°F and bake for 1 hour, or until the cake feels springy to the touch. Flip the pan upside down to cool. As the cake bakes and cools, make sure no loud sounds rattle the cake. Carefully remove the pan, slice, and serve.

JEWISH BUTTER CAKE

(Dutch: Joodse Boterkoeke)

Survivor | **MAX GARCIA**

I created this recipe from memories of my mother making it with and for the family. I started making this butter cake with my mom when I was very young, maybe about ten years old. She was always making Boterkoeke for the family. She was the youngest sister of eight and became a baker for all of the family. Her sisters' friends would always take slices home for their husbands. I was about ten years old when I understood what she was doing and memorized the recipe.

When I was taken to Auschwitz and got accustomed to it, I began to think, How can I remember my mom and our family life? I told myself, Look, the only way you're going to do it is to make Boterkoeke. So I remembered the recipe and continued to make it all these years after Auschwitz. It's a straightforward recipe.

SERVES 16

1 cup (2 sticks) unsalted butter, melted and cooled
½ cup sugar
2 egg yolks (save the whites for the egg wash)
1⅓ cups sifted all-purpose flour
Pinch of salt

Preheat the oven to 325°F and butter the bottom and sides of a 9- or 10-inch round cake pan.

Mix the melted butter, sugar, and egg yolks in a large bowl. Add the flour and salt and stir to combine. Pour the batter into the prepared cake pan.

Add 1 tablespoon of water to the egg whites and beat lightly to make an egg wash. Brush over the top of the batter. Drag the tines of a fork through the egg wash to create a decorative pattern. Bake for 40 minutes or until the top is browned, rotating the pan at least twice (preferably three times) during cooking.

CHOCOLATE CAKE

Survivor | **GOLDIE FINKELSTEIN**

SERVES 16

½ cup vegetable oil, plus more oil, cooking spray, or butter
1 box yellow cake mix
One 3.9-ounce box chocolate pudding mix
1 cup sour cream
4 eggs
1 cup chocolate chips (optional)
1 cup nuts (optional)

Preheat the oven to 350°F and coat a Bundt pan with oil, cooking spray, or butter.

Whisk together cake mix, pudding mix, sour cream, eggs, and ½ cup oil in a large bowl. Fold in chocolate chips or nuts, if using. Pour batter into prepared Bundt pan. Bake for 45 minutes to 1 hour, until a cake tester comes out clean. Cool in the pan for 10 minutes, then turn a cooling rack upside down on top of the pan. Flip the cake and carefully remove it from the pan. Cool completely before serving.

Note: If you plan to use chocolate chips or nuts, roll them in the cake mix residue so they won't fall to the bottom during baking.

CHOCOLATE SYRUP FUDGE CAKE

Survivor | **GOLDIE FINKELSTEIN**

SERVES 20

4 eggs
1 teaspoon vanilla extract
1 cup sugar
½ cup (1 stick) unsalted butter or margarine, softened
1 cup all-purpose flour
2 cups chocolate syrup
1½ teaspoons baking powder

Preheat the oven to 350°F and grease an 8-by-12-inch cake pan with cooking spray.

In a large bowl, combine the eggs, vanilla, sugar, butter, flour, chocolate syrup, and baking powder and mix with an electric mixer for approximately 3 minutes, until well combined. Pour into the prepared cake pan and bake for 45 minutes, or until set. Cool in the pan, then slice and serve.

Note: Parve if margarine is used.

CHOCOLATE SYRUP FUDGE CAKE
IN MEMORY OF MY MOM GOLDIE
- Joe Finkelstein

Ingredients:

4 Eggs
1 tsp. vanilla extract
1 c. sugar
1/2 c. (1 stick) butter or margerine, softened
1 c. flour
2 c. chocolate syrup
1 1/2 tsp. baking powder

Directions:

Preheat oven to 350°F and grease an 8 x 12-inch cake pan with cooking spray.

To a large bowl, add eggs, vanilla, sugar, butter, flour, chocolate syrup, and baking powder. Mix for approximately 3 minutes.

Bake for 45 minutes, or until set.

WHISKEY CAKE

Survivor | **GOLDIE FINKELSTEIN**

SERVES 12–16

FOR THE CAKE:

14-ounce box yellow cake mix
3.2-ounce box vanilla pudding mix
½ cup vegetable oil
1 shot (1–2 ounces) whiskey
1 cup milk
4 eggs

FOR THE GLAZE:

½–1 cup (1–2 sticks) butter or margarine
½ cup whiskey
½ cup sugar

Make the cake: Preheat the oven to 350°F and prepare a Bundt pan with nonstick cooking spray or butter.

In a large bowl, combine the cake mix and pudding mix, oil, whiskey, milk, and eggs. Pour the batter into the prepared pan and bake for about 1 hour, checking for doneness after 45 minutes, until the top is golden and a cake tester or toothpick comes out clean.

Make the glaze: While the cake bakes, combine the butter, whiskey, and sugar in a small saucepan over medium heat. Bring to a boil, stirring frequently, and cook until slightly thickened. Be careful not to let the glaze boil over!

Pour half the hot glaze over the cake while it is still in the pan. Invert the cake onto a cooling rack. Let stand for 30 minutes, then pour on the rest of the glaze.

Note: This cake can be made parve by substituting margarine and cooking spray for butter.

JERBO

(Hungarian: zserbó)

Survivor | **EDITH MORE**

Edith's son, Erwin, recalls: When my mother and I were liberated, I was seventeen years old. We didn't go home; we lived with a cousin in a small village. I had nothing to do, so I was baking. I was cooking. I used to make jerbo—a layered Hungarian confectionery that was popular in Hungary.

YIELDS 12 PIECES

FOR THE DOUGH:

3 cups all-purpose flour, plus more for the work surface
1 tablespoon sugar
Pinch of baking powder (use the tip of a knife)
⅛ teaspoon salt (if you are using only unsalted butter)
1 cup (2 sticks) butter (1 salted, 1 unsalted), cut into pieces and softened
4 egg yolks
1 tablespoon sour cream

Make the dough: In a large mixing bowl, whisk together the flour, sugar, baking powder, and salt, if using only unsalted butter. Add the butter, mix in the egg yolks, then add the sour cream.

Flour a work surface, turn the dough onto the surface, and knead until smooth. Cut the dough into thirds, shape into balls, and wrap each in plastic wrap. Refrigerate for at least 1 hour or overnight.

When ready to assemble, preheat the oven to 350°F and remove the dough to soften at room temperature until rollable but still cool.

FOR THE FILLING AND TOPPING:

12 ounces walnuts, finely ground
5 tablespoons sugar, or to taste
1 cup raspberry jam, preferably seeded
5 ounces bittersweet chocolate, chopped
2 tablespoons unsalted butter

Make the filling: In a small bowl, combine the walnuts and sugar. Set aside.

On a floured work surface, roll out the first dough ball to approximately ¼ inch thick and large enough to cover the bottom of a half-sheet pan (approximately 9 by 13 inches). Place the dough on the ungreased pan and cover with half of the raspberry jam. Sprinkle half of the walnut and sugar mixture over the jam. Repeat with the second dough ball, placing it on top of the first layer of dough and topping with the remainder of the jam and walnut mixture. Roll out the third dough ball and use it to cover the two previous layers. Score the dough all over with the tip of a sharp knife or fork.

Bake for approximately 45 minutes, or until golden. Remove from the oven and set aside to cool completely.

Make the topping: While you wait, warm the chocolate in a double boiler. When it begins to melt, add the butter and stir to combine. Cool slightly, then spread over the top of the cooled pastry. Leave at room temperature for several hours or overnight to set, then slice diagonally into diamond-shaped jerbo. Serve.

HOLIDAY DISHES

מנות לארוחות חג

LATKES IN THE WIESEL FAMILY TRADITION

In Memory of | **ELIE WIESEL**

(submitted by Mrs. Marion Wiesel)

Elie Wiesel's family latkes recipe has been shared lovingly with a dear family friend, Ronald S. Lauder. As Marion Wiesel says, it's simple and easy.

SERVES 4–5

3–4 baking potatoes, peeled
3 eggs, beaten
1 cup all-purpose flour
1 teaspoon salt
Pinch of ground black pepper
High-grade oil for frying
Important: no onion; no garlic

Grate potatoes finely into a bowl. Add cold water to the bowl. Mix and drain extra liquid. Combine potatoes, eggs, flour, salt, and pepper. Mix well. Heat a half inch of oil over medium-high heat in a large frying pan. Use a tablespoon to drop the potato mixture into the hot oil, one at a time. Cook until browned and crunchy, turning as necessary to brown both sides. Remove latkes, place on paper towels to drain. Serve with applesauce or sour cream.

Latkes in the Wiesel Family Tradition
(Simple and Easy)

3-4 baking potatoes, peeled
3 eggs, beaten
1 cup all purpose flour
1 tsp salt
high-grade oil for frying
pinch of ground black pepper
Important: no onion, no garlic

1. Grate potatoes finely into a bowl
2. Add cold water to the bowl
3. Mix and drain extra liquid
4. Combine potatoes, eggs, flour, salt & pepper. Mix well.
5. Heat a half inch of oil over medium-high heat in a large frying pan
6. Use tablespoon to drop potato mixture into hot oil, one at a time
7. Cook until browned and crunchy, turning as necessary to brown both sides
8. Remove latkes, place on paper towels to drain
9. Serve with applesauce or sour cream

POTATO KUGEL WITH MATZO MEAL

Survivor | **RUTH WEBBER**

(submitted in memory of Malka "Molly" Muschkies, her mother)

This is my mother's recipe. It's how potato kugel used to be: dense, but not dry and not crisp on the top. This is the recipe that I used to do. Now I make an easier one.

SERVES 12–16

10 large potatoes
3 large onions, finely grated
1 cup oil
1 cup flour
2 tablespoons matzo meal
3 teaspoons baking powder
2½ teaspoons salt
6 large eggs (or 7 medium)

Preheat the oven to 350°F and grease a 9-by-13-inch baking dish thoroughly with oil.

Peel the potatoes and grate them into a colander, tossing with the salt, to allow some of the water to drain. Add drained potatoes to a large bowl with grated onions, oil, flour, matzo meal, and baking powder. Lightly beat the eggs and add them to the bowl, stirring to combine.

Set the baking dish in the preheated oven for a few minutes to warm, then pour in the mixture and add additional oil on top. Bake for 1½ hours or until nicely browned. Remove and cover with foil or wax paper until cool.

Note: This potato kugel is not kosher for Passover.

CHAROSET

Survivor | **RUTH WEBBER**

Charoset is a sweet dish made from chopped nuts, fruit, wine, and honey. It is traditionally served as part of the Passover Seder plate. In Ashkenazi Jewish households, charoset is made with apples and cinnamon; among Sephardim, it is made from raisins, figs, or dates.

I recommend using any tart, firm apples for this recipe. I prefer Granny Smith apples (do not use Red or Golden Delicious or McIntosh Red). Also, I like to use sweet Manischewitz wine.

SERVES 4–6

2 apples, grated or diced
1 cup chopped walnuts (see note)
4 teaspoons sweet red wine
2 teaspoons ground cinnamon
2 teaspoons honey
1 lemon, cut in half

Mix the apples, walnuts, wine, cinnamon, and honey. Squeeze in the juice of half a lemon and taste for tartness. Add more juice as needed (we like the charoset to be tart, but the amount of juice depends on the sweetness of the apples).

Note: Before preparing the charoset, freshen the walnuts in the oven so that they are nice and crisp. Spread them out on a cookie sheet and bake at 350°F for 5 to 10 minutes, then wrap in a dish towel and rub to remove the skins.

GEFILTE FISH

Survivor | **EUGENE GINTER**
(submitted in honor of his wife, Rachelle Ginter)

My mother would go to the fish store and pick the fish that looked healthy, insisting on Michigan whitefish. In Poland, before the war, my grandmother would buy live fish. She would put a wad of cotton soaked with vodka in the fish's mouth. Then she would remove the cotton and put the fish in the bathtub until she was ready to cook it.

I shared this recipe with my wife, Rachelle. She only makes it at Passover because it is so much work to prepare.

After the war, we ate to live, not lived to eat. Because what happened was, I lost my parents twice. Once in the war when they took me away from my mother. Then they took my father away from me. Then I was in an orphanage for months. I didn't have a mother for almost a year until she found me after the war. The fact that we were together was more important to me than what was put on the table.

SERVES 12–16

6 to 8 pounds ground fish (reserve the bones, head, and skin)
4 large onions, 1 grated and 3 peeled and quartered
3 eggs
1 teaspoon salt, plus more to taste
¼ cup sugar, plus more if needed
5 tablespoons matzo meal, plus more if needed
4 carrots, cut into rounds
Freshly ground black pepper
Lettuce leaves, for serving

Place the ground fish in a large bowl. Add the grated onion, eggs, salt, and sugar and mix well. Add enough matzo meal to make a light, soft mixture. If the consistency seems thin, add additional matzo meal, plus additional sugar to taste. Using a soupspoon or your hands, form the mixture into 3-inch-long oval-shaped balls.

Fill a large pot with water and bring to a boil over medium-high heat. You do not want to crowd the fish balls in the pot, so depending upon the size of your pot, you may need to place another pot of water on the stove as well. Gently drop the fish balls into the boiling water, making sure the water covers the fish. Add the quartered onions and carrots and season with salt and pepper, then return to a boil. Cover and lower the heat so the broth just barely simmers. Cook for 1½ hours, then uncover and simmer for another 30 minutes, or until the liquid is reduced. Remove the fish balls and carrots.

While the fish balls are cooking, put the fish bones,

head, and skin in another large pot, add water to cover, and cook over low heat for 2 hours. Remove and discard the fish head. Strain the broth, pressing on the skin and bones to get as much of the flavor out as possible. Discard the skin and bones. Add the strained fish broth to the reduced broth in the first pot. Let cool.

When cool, mix in a blender to create a thick sauce (it will look like gelatin). Serve each fish ball on a bed of lettuce garnished with a carrot slice and a spoonful of the sauce.

Note: Ask your fishmonger to grind the fish, reserving the bones, head, and skin. The mixture should be half pike and half whitefish. The amounts for the rest of the ingredients remain the same even if you use the lesser weight of fish.

JARRED GEFILTE FISH

Survivor | **RUTH WEBBER**

(submitted in memory of Malka "Molly" Muschkies, her mother)

My mother picked up this unique recipe from my grandmother. I come from Ostrowiec, Poland. When the Germans came, within a short time they formed a ghetto, and they were not very nice to the Jews. They were not very gentle to older people. My grandmother was always a weak person, and my mother decided that she needed to help my grandparents out because they didn't have any means. They couldn't do anything because they were very sick, and bad things were happening to them. My mother was always at their house, and she took over the cooking and housekeeping. She would feed them not only whatever food they had, but she also bought food and prepared it the way my grandmother wanted. And the gefilte fish was one of the dishes she made. As long as we were in the ghetto, my mother was doing that. Then there were rumors that there would be a problem with the ghetto, that Germans were going to liquidate it. And we knew already from other cities what that meant.

YIELDS ABOUT 35–40 PIECES

FOR THE FISH STOCK:

4 onions, sliced
1 piece of carp, or any fish whole
Fish bones and fish heads (The fish market has them. The more the better.)
3 tablespoons salt, plus more for fish
4 carrots, sliced
1 teaspoon ground white pepper
5 tablespoons sugar
10–12 cups water, or more if needed

Prepare the stock: Rinse the onions, carp, and bones and heads well, then salt them and wrap in a cheesecloth. Chill the cheesecloth packet in the refrigerator for a few hours or overnight.

Place the chilled cheesecloth packet on the bottom of a large pot. On top of the cheesecloth, arrange the 4 sliced carrots in a thick layer. You put the carrots on top of the pile of ingredients so that when you are done cooking, you can remove the carrots easily, before you take anything else out of the pot. You use the carrots to garnish the gefilte fish, so you don't want the carrots to get mixed up in the stock.

Add the 3 tablespoons salt, white pepper, and sugar to the pot and cover with at least 10 to 12 cups of water. If using extra bones and heads, use more water and adjust the seasonings. Boil for 1½ hours, then remove the carrots and set aside to use as a garnish. Remove the

FOR THE FISH:

6 pounds ground fish (3 pounds whitefish, 1½ pounds pickerel, and 1½ pounds pike or trout)
5 teaspoons salt
½ teaspoon pepper
6 tablespoons sugar
1 parsnip, grated
3 onions, grated
6 eggs
4 tablespoons matzo meal
1 cup very cold water (ice water is fine)

cheesecloth packet, then strain the stock to remove any impurities. Set aside.

There are two ways to prepare the fish balls:

Ruth's method: I use a large, heavy-duty electric mixer to combine everything. Put the ground fish into the bowl and mix on low speed (setting 2 or 3). Slowly add the salt, pepper, sugar, parsnip, and onions. Alternate adding the eggs and the matzo meal, then add cold water, a little at a time.

Molly's method: My mother used to place the fish in a chopping bowl and add the eggs, water, sugar, salt, pepper, matzo meal, parsnip, and onions, then chop until blended lightly and smoothly.

Whichever method you choose, set the fish mixture aside to chill for 15 to 30 minutes, or in the refrigerator overnight. Moisten hands and shape the chilled mixture into balls of your desired size.

Bring the clear stock to a boil, then add the prepared fish balls. Cover and return the stock to a boil, then reduce the heat to low and simmer gently for 2 to 2½ hours, checking occasionally and adding water as necessary. Adjust seasoning to taste. I know people don't like to taste raw fish anymore because they don't think it's healthy, but you need to know whether the fish needs more salt, pepper, or sugar. So, I keep tasting the fish stock that the gefilte fish cooks in, and I adjust according to what I taste.

Cool in the pot slightly before removing fish balls to a platter or glass jar. Garnish the fish with the slices of carrots and the broth.

Note: The amounts for the stock will depend on the amount of fish used. You don't have to make the fish all at once. You can make the stock ahead of time—mix the fish in the morning and cook it in the stock at night. Mother made the fish ahead of time and stored it in sterilized jars until she needed it. I do that too. I use clean glass jars with secure covers and make the fish 3 to 4 days ahead of time, and it keeps very well. But once you open the jar, you have to use the fish within a day or two.

STUFFED GEFILTE FISH

Survivor | **RACHEL ROTH**

"While imprisoned in Majdanek, Rachel always told stories to the other women in her barrack. She used the art of storytelling as a way to distract the women from their hunger and the many horrors they witnessed throughout the day. Rachel would tell the women stories of the wonderful Jewish meals she once had in her house. 'Attractively decorated with slices of carrot, the gefilte fish served in a sweet sauce is excellent. The wonderful aroma of a roast wafts in from the kitchen. The long white noodles swim in the yellow broth.' Through the use of figurative language, Rachel was able to activate the other prisoners' senses of taste, smell, and sight, which served as a distraction for them."[1]

Years later, Rachel's son recalls, she was very proud to be able to serve this gefilte fish to the Chief Rabbi of Israel, who dined with the family in their home.

SERVES 10–12

FOR THE POACHING LIQUID:

10 cups cold water, or enough to cover the fish
2 carrots, thinly sliced into rounds
2 small white onions, diced
½ teaspoon ground black pepper
1 teaspoon salt
1–2 tablespoons sugar, to taste

FOR THE STUFFING:

1 pound ground fish (carp, pike, whitefish, or a combination)

Prepare the poaching liquid and the stuffing: Add the cold water, carrots, onions, pepper, salt, and sugar to a soup pot, stir, and set aside. In a large mixing bowl, combine the ground fish, onions, eggs, matzo meal, salt, pepper, and sugar. Mix well.

To make only the patties: With wet hands, shape the fish mixture into oblong patties and arrange in the pot with the cold poaching liquid. When all the fish is shaped, place the pot over medium heat, bring to a simmer, slightly open the cover, and let cook for 1½ hours.

To make traditional stuffed fish: Prepare the patties as described above, using 2 eggs in the mixture instead of one. Arrange the slices of carp so they lay flat on your cutting surface. Form the patties large enough to fill each slice, then stuff one into the center of each slice. The patties will expand and stay in the slices of fish.

1 Jessica Catanzaro and Theresa Reed, "Ruchama Rachel Rothstein (Rachel Roth)," Wagner College Holocaust Center, April 2015, https://faculty.wagner.edu/lori-weintrob/ruchama-rachel-rothstein-rachel-roth/.

2 small white onions, grated
2 large eggs (1 egg if you are only making the patties)
½ cup matzo meal
1 teaspoon salt
¼ teaspoon ground black pepper
2 tablespoons sugar
One 2-pound carp, scaled, deboned, and cut into 1- to 2-inch-thick slices
Prepared horseradish, for serving

Note: Most people are familiar with the stuffing served as patties or balls. This recipe is the original fish with stuffing. Feel free to make patties only.

Carefully arrange the stuffed fish slices in the pot and cover with the cold poaching liquid. When all the fish is prepared, place the pot over medium heat and bring to a simmer. Uncover slightly to vent and let cook for 2 hours.

The fish is ready when the poaching liquid darkens. Promptly remove the stuffed fish slices or the patties from the pot and chill them in the refrigerator until serving.

Make the jelly: Remove the cooked carrots from the pot and strain the poaching liquid into a storage container. Discard the onions and other solids. Refrigerate the liquid until it congeals into a jelly.

To serve: Arrange 1 patty or slice of stuffed fish on each small plate and garnish with cooked carrots. Serve cold with 1 to 2 tablespoons of the jelly and some horseradish.

PASSOVER ROLLS

Survivor | **RACHEL ROTH**

Rachel's children, Ram Roth and David and Leah Chencinski, recall: One of the most popular things our mother made was Passover bilkeluch (rolls). They tasted great warm right out of the oven, and they were even better when we sliced them in half and added some butter, which melted. Our mom would make them fresh on Yom Tov (not sabbath), and family and guests would have them plain while hot.

If there were any leftovers, they cooled down and would last for days, making excellent Pesach sandwiches. We even grabbed them plain or with butter or cheese or as snacks while traveling with the family on Hol Hamoed. For a fleishig meal, we would eat the rolls with chicken fat.

YIELDS 12 ROLLS

2 cups matzo meal
3 tablespoons sugar
1 teaspoon salt
1 cup water
½ cup vegetable oil
4 eggs

Preheat the oven to 375°F.

Combine the matzo meal, sugar, and salt in a large heat-proof bowl. In a small saucepan, bring the water and oil to a boil and pour the hot liquid over the dry ingredients. Stir vigorously but carefully to avoid scalding yourself. Add the eggs one at a time, continuing to stir until well combined.

Spray your hands with a bit of nonstick cooking spray and form the mixture into twelve 2- to 3-inch balls. Bake on an ungreased cookie sheet for 50 minutes, or until golden and cooked through.

PASSOVER KNISHES

Survivor | **GOLDIE FINKELSTEIN**

You can make this dish vegetarian by substituting mushrooms for the liver.

YIELDS 12 PIECES

2 pounds baking potatoes, such as russet or white
5 tablespoons margarine or butter, 3 tablespoons of it melted
2 eggs, lightly beaten
1 cup matzo meal
1 teaspoon salt
½ teaspoon ground black pepper
8 ounces chicken liver, or 8 ounces mushrooms, finely chopped
1 egg yolk plus 1 teaspoon water, for brushing

Preheat the oven to 400°F.

Place the potatoes in a saucepan with water to cover, put on medium heat, and bring to a boil. Cook the potatoes, turning occasionally, until they can be easily pierced with a knife. Drain the potatoes and when they are cool enough to handle, peel and mash them. Measure out 3 cups of the mashed potatoes and let cool completely.

In a large bowl, combine 3 cups mashed potatoes with 3 tablespoons melted margarine, eggs, matzo meal, salt, and pepper. Mix until smooth.

Form the potato mixture into small balls about 3 inches in diameter. Press a 1-inch indentation into the center of each ball with your thumb to create a space for the filling.

In a large pan over medium heat, melt the remaining 2 tablespoons margarine. Add the liver (or mushrooms if using instead) and sauté, stirring occasionally, about 5 minutes. Remove the liver to a cutting board and chop finely. (If using mushrooms, cook until they have browned and almost all their moisture has evaporated, about 10 minutes.) Drain or pat dry and set aside to cool.

Place 1 teaspoon of the filling into the cavity of each knish. (You may pinch the dough around the filling to seal it shut, or you may keep the knish open so the filling shows.) Place the knishes on a greased cookie sheet or baking pan. Brush each knish with the mixture of egg yolk and water. Bake for 20 minutes. Let cool for 5 to 10 minutes before serving.

LEA'S PASSOVER NOODLES

Survivor | **LEA ROTH**

At home, we made potato starch from scratch. When we grated potatoes for a kugel, there was a buildup of wet starch that stayed at the bottom of the bowl. This mixture would be dried and used as potato starch. Today, it is easier to go to the store and buy the starch already made.

I have always preferred making my food to getting the ready-made. That included making my noodles for the holidays. It was tedious but very much worth it. Making these noodles has become a family Passover tradition. Before the war, in Europe, we had no store-bought goods. And now the homemade noodles taste better than anything you could get at the store.

SERVES 12

5 eggs
1½ cups potato starch
2 cups water

Beat the eggs, then beat in the potato starch, and then add the water. Stir until there are no lumps. The mixture should be thin, like a crepe batter.

Lightly grease a frying pan and pour in enough of the batter to just cover the entire surface. Cook for 1 minute until set, then carefully flip and cook for an additional minute. Remove the crepe from the pan and set aside. Repeat until all the batter is used.

When slightly cooled, cut each crepe into long strips. The noodles can accompany soup or be served as a side dish.

Note: The strips should be pretty thin, approximately half an inch.

PASSOVER NOODLES

Survivors | **FRIEDA AND SAM WEINREICH**

Sam and Frieda's daughter Marilyn says: This is an old Passover family recipe. I continue to make these noodles for my family. All three generations love them! When I make these egg noodles, I put some oil on a paper towel and wipe it on a nonstick pan. I make crepe-like pancakes, then stack them and cut them into ¼-inch strips.

You can make these ahead of time and freeze them in baggie meal portions to make life simpler. I know I'm frantically busy on the day of the Seder when I first need them, and I am happy to make them ahead of time since they are pretty time-consuming to make.

SERVES 6–10

8 eggs
½ cup water
2 tablespoons potato starch
Dash of salt
About 2 teaspoons oil

In a large bowl, whisk the eggs, then whisk in the water. Whisk in the potato starch and salt to incorporate.

Rub an 8-inch nonstick frying pan with oil and heat. When hot, drop a ladleful of the noodle batter into the pan (enough to coat the bottom) and tilt to coat the surface completely. When set, after about 1 minute, carefully flip the crepe and cook the other side, about another minute. Remove to a cutting board and repeat, adding more oil to coat the pan, until all the batter is used. Cut the crepes into thin strips to use as noodles in chicken soup, or freeze individual portions for later use.

CHALLAH

Survivor | **EVA SZEPESI**

Eva's daughter Anita shares that her mother loves the smell that permeates the whole apartment when the family bakes challah.

Three generations—Eva, Anita, and Anita's daughter Celina—baked the challah together. Since Celina has moved to study in Vienna, baking has sustained a special connection between the women. Every Shabbat, they always send each other photos of their homemade challah.

This year, the three generations baked the round challah for Rosh Hashanah together at home. Anita reminisces that it was extraordinary for Eva to be able to bake together with her granddaughter again.

SERVES 10

2 cups lukewarm water
¼-ounce package active dry yeast
2 eggs, beaten
6 tablespoons sunflower oil
½ cup sugar
1 tablespoon salt
About 8 cups all-purpose flour, plus more for kneading
1 egg yolk, beaten
Sesame or poppy seeds, for sprinkling

Pour the lukewarm water into a mixing bowl. Add the yeast and leave for 10 minutes. Add 2 eggs, oil, sugar, and salt and whisk to blend. Add the flour, ½ cup at a time, stirring each time you add more flour. When it becomes too thick to stir, knead with your hands for about 10 minutes, until the dough is smooth, elastic, and not sticky.

Shape the dough into a ball. Coat with oil, cover with a clean kitchen towel, and let rise for 50 minutes, or until the dough doubles in size. Punch down the dough to remove air pockets. Let rise for another 50 minutes, or until doubled in size. Punch the dough down again and move it to a floured work surface. Knead for a few minutes, adding more flour as needed to keep the dough from feeling sticky.

Preheat the oven to 350°F and line a baking sheet with parchment paper.

Braid the dough into a round shape and let rise for 30 minutes. Brush with egg yolk and sprinkle sesame or poppy seeds on top. Bake for 30 minutes, or until the top is browned and the loaf makes a hollow sound when tapped on the bottom. Let cool, then slice and serve.

CARROT TZIMMES

Survivor | **TOVA FRIEDMAN**

You have to understand that I have no memories before the war because I was only a year old, so my memory of food is really after the war, after liberation. We were liberated from Auschwitz in 1945 and went back to our hometown in Poland. Food was, of course, scarce, so I can't even talk about recipes there because we barely had anything to eat even after the war.

I first remember the food in a displaced persons camp in Germany. There, my mother began to cook from what she remembered. One of the things that I remember more than anything else was her tzimmes because it contained sugar; it was sweet. It was like eating dessert. I was about ten or eleven years old. I remember this exceptionally well. For Shabbos, she would make the tzimmes. It's a stewed carrot dish that is traditionally served with the Rosh Hashanah meal, when it is customary to eat sweet foods for the new year.

SERVES: 6

- 2½ pounds carrots, cleaned, peeled, and sliced into ½-inch disks
- ½ cup honey
- 2 tablespoons brown sugar
- 1½ teaspoons vegetable oil
- ½ cup white or golden raisins
- ½ cup pitted prunes
- ½ lemon rind, grated
- ½ teaspoon grated fresh ginger

Set up a steamer basket over a pot of simmering water. Add the carrots and steam for 15 minutes.

Remove the steamer basket from the pot, drain all but about ½ cup of the steaming water, and transfer the carrots to the pot. Turn the heat to medium and add the honey, brown sugar, and oil and cook until the liquid thickens and glazes the carrots, about 20 minutes. Add the raisins, prunes, lemon rind, and ginger and stir well. Cook for another 10 minutes, or until the mixture is almost dry.

Note: All quantities subject to taste. Do not burn the carrots!

HAZELNUT SANDWICH COOKIES

Survivor | **RUTH WEBBER**

I bake these cookies for my whole family. I recommend buying already skinned hazelnuts to make the job easier. Otherwise, you will need to roast them in a skillet or on a pan in the oven—then roll them to get the skins off (too much work!).

YIELDS 42 COOKIES

FOR THE COOKIES:

2 cups skinned hazelnuts
1 cup sugar
1 cup (2 sticks) unsalted pareve (Passover) margarine, at room temperature
4 large egg whites, at room temperature
6 tablespoons matzo cake meal
6 tablespoons potato starch

FOR THE FILLING:

4 tablespoons pareve margarine, at room temperature
6 ounces pareve semisweet chocolate, chopped or chips

Preheat the oven to 350°F and place oven racks on the middle and lowest settings. Line two cookie sheets with parchment paper.

Make the cookies: Put the nuts and sugar in a food processor and pulse until the mixture resembles coarse meal.

In the bowl of an electric mixer, beat the margarine until light and creamy. Add the nut-sugar mixture and beat until well mixed and light. Add the egg whites and beat for about 3 minutes more, until very fluffy. Sift the cake meal and potato starch together and stir gently into the egg mixture until no dry ingredients are visible.

Using a rounded measuring teaspoon, form the dough into mounds, about the size of a marble, and place them about 2 inches apart on the prepared cookie sheets. Make the mounds as round as possible so that they will fit together nicely when you assemble them into sandwiches. Place on the middle rack in the oven and bake for 10 to 20 minutes, until the edges are well browned. If using two racks, switch the cookie sheets every 5 minutes so that the cookies bake evenly. (The time may vary depending on the type of oven, type of cookie sheet, and how many sheets you are using.)

Carefully lift the parchment paper onto a cooling rack and allow the cookies to cool completely. They should be crisp when cool; if not, return them to the oven for 5 minutes.

Make the filling: Bring 2 inches of water to boil in the

bottom of a double boiler or in a pot. Meanwhile, chop the margarine into 1-inch chunks.

When the water comes to a boil, remove from the heat. Place the chocolate and margarine in the top of the double boiler, or in a metal or heat-safe glass bowl set in the pot, over the hot water but not touching it. Stir until the chocolate-butter mixture is melted and smooth. Set aside to cool to room temperature.

To assemble, spread the flat side of a cookie with a thin layer of chocolate and top with the flat side of another cookie. Repeat with the remaining cookies.

Note: The dough can be made ahead and kept in the refrigerator for 1 day or frozen for up to 3 months.

PASSOVER NUT COOKIES

Survivor | **GOLDIE FINKELSTEIN**

The cookie dough can be made ahead and frozen. Just take out one log at a time, slice, and bake.

YIELDS 24 COOKIES

½ cup (1 stick) butter, softened, plus more for greasing the pans
¾ cup sugar
2 eggs
½ cup chopped walnuts
¾ cup matzo cake meal
¼ cup potato starch
2 tablespoons lemon or orange juice
Pinch of salt

In a large bowl, cream the butter and sugar. Add the eggs, nuts, cake meal, potato starch, juice, and salt. Mix well to form a dough.

Divide dough into several logs about 2 inches in diameter. Wrap in wax paper and refrigerate overnight.

Preheat the oven to 350°F. Grease two cookie sheets.

Remove the chilled dough from the wax paper, cut it into ¼-inch slices, and place on the prepared cookie sheets, leaving equal spaces between. Bake for 20 to 22 minutes until set and lightly browned.

FARFEL COOKIES

Survivors | **FRIEDA AND SAM WEINREICH**

Sam and Frieda's daughter Marilyn recalls: This is an old Passover family recipe. We have made and loved these cookies for decades. My family likes to use regular Passover cottonseed oil when we make these cookies. It works with the recipe. They come out delicious, and my family enjoys them.

YIELDS 24 COOKIES

2 cups matzo meal
2 cups matzo farfel
1 1/4 cups sugar
2/3 cup vegetable oil
4 eggs, beaten
1 cup chopped pecans
1 teaspoon ground cinnamon

Combine all ingredients in a large bowl and mix thoroughly to form a dough. Cover and refrigerate for 1 hour.

Preheat the oven to 350°F. Grease a cookie sheet and line it with parchment paper. Form the dough into teaspoon-size balls. Arrange them on the sheet and flatten the balls slightly. Bake for 20 to 25 minutes, or until set and lightly browned. Cool on the sheets set on a wire rack.

PASSOVER FUDGIES

Survivor | **GOLDIE FINKELSTEIN**

YIELDS 24 BARS

4 eggs
2 cups sugar
1 cup (2 sticks) butter, melted and cooled
1/2 teaspoon vanilla extract
6 tablespoons matzo cake meal
1 cup cocoa powder
1 cup nuts of choice, coarsely chopped

Preheat the oven to 375°F and lightly grease a 9-by-13-inch baking pan.

In a large bowl, beat the eggs. Add sugar gradually, mixing to combine, then add the butter and vanilla. Beat well.

In a separate bowl, sift together the cake meal and cocoa powder and add to the wet ingredients, mixing to combine. Stir in the nuts.

Pour the batter into the prepared pan and bake for 20 to 25 minutes, until set. Cool and cut into bars to serve.

FRUIT KUGEL

(Yiddish: frukht kugl)

Survivor | **RUTH WEBBER**

This fruit kugel has always been one of my family's favorite recipes. The fruit is the star of this kugel (we are a big fruit-eating family!), with the nuts and cinnamon enhancing it. I like to use Granny Smith apples for this recipe. However, any tart, firm apple would work (not McIntosh).

SERVES 12–18

½ cup vegetable oil, plus more for greasing the pan
6 eggs
1 cup water
1 cup matzo meal
¾ cup sugar
1 teaspoon ground cinnamon
3 baking apples
1 cup chopped nuts of choice
11 ounces mixed dried fruit, diced
7 ounces dried peaches, diced

Preheat the oven to 325°F and grease a 9-by-13-inch baking dish.

Beat the eggs and water in a large bowl until well combined. Beat in the matzo meal, add sugar and cinnamon, and mix to combine.

Peel and grate the apples into a separate bowl, then add the nuts and dried fruit and toss to combine. Stir in the ½ cup oil. Add the apple mixture to the matzo mixture and mix until the fruit and nuts are evenly distributed. Pour the batter into the prepared pan. Bake for 1 hour, or until set and golden brown.

CHOCOLATE GRAND MARNIER TORTE

Survivor | **RUTH WEBBER**

This chocolate cake is my favorite dessert. It is relatively simple. What makes this recipe unique is its beautiful presentation. You can serve it on a raspberry sauce or other kind of sauce—use your imagination. I like to use unsweetened chocolate to make this cake.

SERVES 10–12

FOR THE TORTE:

1 cup (2 sticks) butter, plus more for greasing the pan
5 eggs
10 ounces semisweet or bittersweet chocolate
2 ounces (2 squares) unsweetened chocolate, chopped
¼ cup Grand Marnier or other orange-flavored liqueur
Whipped cream, for serving

FOR THE RASPBERRY SAUCE:

Two 12-ounce bags frozen unsweetened raspberries, thawed
¾ cup confectioners' sugar
2 tablespoons raspberry Grand Marnier or other liqueur of your choice

Preheat the oven to 400°F. Butter an 8-inch springform pan, line the sides with parchment, and grease the paper.

Make the torte: Place the eggs into a bowl of very hot water and let stand for 5 minutes. Meanwhile, in a 2-quart glass bowl, heat the chocolates and 1 cup butter in a microwave oven on high, 2½ to 3 minutes, stirring twice, until melted and smooth. Set aside to cool slightly.

Crack the warmed eggs into a large bowl and beat with an electric mixer on high speed until thick and light yellow, about 5 minutes. Add the chocolate mixture and Grand Marnier and beat until well blended.

Pour the batter into the prepared pan. Bake for 15 to 18 minutes, or until almost set. Let cool for 1 hour, then cover with foil and refrigerate for several hours, until firm. Remove the torte from the refrigerator at least 1 hour before serving.

Make the raspberry sauce: Blend the raspberries and confectioners' sugar in a food processor. Add the raspberry Grand Marnier and blend well. To remove any seeds, press the pureed mixture through a fine-mesh strainer set over a stainless steel or glass bowl. Scrape the underside of the strainer with a rubber spatula. Discard the seeds. If not serving the sauce immediately, cover and refrigerate for up to 2 days. Stir before using.

Run a sharp knife around the edges of the torte and remove the sides of the pan. Cut into slices and serve each slice in a pool of raspberry sauce. Top with whipped cream.

FLOURLESS CHOCOLATE TORTE

Survivor | **EDITH MORE**

This cake is gluten-free and kosher for Passover, but it is not parve.

SERVES 8

- ½ cup (1 stick) unsalted butter, at room temperature, plus more for greasing the pan (optional)
- 5 ounces bittersweet chocolate, preferably Belgian, chopped
- ¼ cup granulated sugar
- 4 eggs, separated
- 1 teaspoon vanilla extract
- 1 tablespoon brown sugar
- Fresh raspberries or other berries of choice (optional, for serving)

Preheat the oven to 350°F and grease a 9-inch cake pan with nonstick cooking spray or softened butter.

Melt the butter and chocolate together in a double boiler. Add the granulated sugar and stir until dissolved. Remove from heat and let cool slightly. Add the egg yolks gradually, one by one, mixing well after each addition. Stir in the vanilla. Remove from heat and set aside.

In a medium bowl, beat the egg whites until foamy. Add the brown sugar and beat until soft peaks form. Fold the whites into the chocolate mixture. Pour the batter into the prepared cake pan and set inside a large, deep-walled casserole dish. Place the dish into the preheated oven and fill the larger pan with boiling water, enough to reach the sides of the cake pan. Bake for about 30 minutes or until firmly set. Cool and slice to serve. Add berries or fruit, if desired.

EASY PASSOVER SPONGE CAKE

Survivor | **RUTH WEBBER**

This is a simple cake meant for informal family gatherings, not for guests. I have this cake finished in advance of the Seder preparations. We nibble on it as we get everything ready. I like to use almonds and sweet Manischewitz wine for this recipe.

If the sponge cake happens to collapse, it's OK. You now have a zakalec, which was a delicacy for my grandson Mark, when my sponge cake occasionally collapsed and I allowed him to feast on it. Zakalec is a cake that doesn't rise properly—so it becomes very dense. I make this in a tube pan and then invert the cake onto a wine-bottle neck to cool.

SERVES 10–12

9 eggs
1½ cups sugar
¼ cup sweet wine, at room temperature
Pinch of salt
½ cup matzo cake meal
½ cup potato starch
½ cup blanched almonds, finely chopped

Preheat the oven to 350°F and grease a tube pan.

In the bowl of an electric mixer, beat the eggs on medium speed for 10 to 15 minutes, until very light and fluffy. Add the remaining ingredients in the order listed, one at a time, beating well after each addition.

Pour into the prepared tube pan and bake for 1 hour, or until the cake springs back when touched. Flip the pan upside down to cool completely, then remove the cake from the pan.

PASSOVER COFFEE CAKE

Survivors | **FRIEDA AND SAM WEINREICH**

Sam and Frieda's daughter Marilyn recalls: This is an old Passover family recipe. We usually make two of these for the holidays and then eat them for breakfast. It's that delicious. I usually give some to my friends, and they all love it.

I use approximately ¼ cup of the called-for sugar when beating the egg whites to keep them from falling. I like stiff peaks. Do not omit any of the ingredients I listed.

SERVES 12–20

FOR THE COFFEE CAKE:

6 eggs, separated
1 cup sugar
½ cup vegetable oil
1 tablespoon vanilla sugar or extract
1½ cups matzo cake meal
1 tablespoon baking powder
Dash of salt
½ cup orange juice

FOR THE TOPPING:

¼ cup sugar
1 teaspoon ground cinnamon
½ cup chopped pecans or other nuts

Preheat the oven to 350°F and grease a 9-by-13-inch pan with nonstick cooking spray.

Make the coffee cake: In a large bowl, beat the egg whites with ¼ cup of the sugar until soft peaks form. In a separate bowl, beat the yolks with the remaining ¾ cup sugar. Add the oil and the vanilla sugar and mix to combine. Sift the cake meal together with the baking powder and salt and add to the yolk mixture, alternating with the orange juice. With a spatula, fold in the egg whites.

Make the topping: In a small bowl, whisk the sugar and cinnamon. Pour the batter into the prepared pan and sprinkle with the cinnamon-sugar mixture and the nuts. Bake for 40 minutes, or until golden brown and set. Cool in the pan before cutting and serving.

Note: This recipe calls for baking powder, which some Jewish families omit during Passover.

CHEWY HONEY CAKE

Survivor | **MIRIAM ZIEGLER**

Miriam's daughter Debbie recalls: For every holiday, except for Pesach, Mom makes the honey cake. That was my Bubbe's recipe. We were reminiscing yesterday about how when Bubbe was already sick and old, she sat at her kitchen table making this cake for us. And there were no measuring cups, no teaspoons—I mean, everything was just thrown in and mixed. We asked, "How many cups was that, Bubbe?" "Three handfuls." So I took everything she used and measured it so that we would have it. And that's the recipe we use.

What makes this cake particularly delicious is how moist and chewy it is—a delightful, simple cake with a rich honey flavor. While the cola in the recipe seems a bit unusual, we like to add it to give the cake a darker color and a caramel flavor.

SERVES 12–20

Juice and zest of 1 orange
1 cup packed dark brown sugar
About 4 cups honey
¾ cup vegetable oil
3 large eggs
1 tablespoon ground cinnamon
3 teaspoons instant coffee granules
3 teaspoons baking cocoa
Pinch of salt
½ teaspoon baking soda
3 teaspoons baking powder
3 cups all-purpose flour
½ cup cola
1 cup raisins or glazed fruit (optional)
½ cup whole almonds (optional)

Preheat the oven to 350°F and line a 12-by-16-inch baking pan (or two 8-inch rounds) with parchment paper.

In the bowl of an electric mixer, combine the orange juice and zest with the sugar, honey, oil, and eggs and mix on medium speed until well blended. With the mixer running, add the cinnamon, coffee, cocoa, salt, baking soda, and baking powder, one after the other. Then add the flour and cola alternately, mixing to incorporate. If desired, stir in the raisins and almonds.

Pour the batter into the prepared pan and bake on the middle rack for 1 hour. Test for doneness by inserting a toothpick in the center of the cake. If it comes out clean, the cake is ready. Place on a wire rack upright to cool.

Once cool, lift the cake out of the pan, put it upside down, and peel the parchment paper off. Wrap tightly in aluminum foil until serving. Serve at room temperature. You can also store the honey cake in the refrigerator or cut, wrap in aluminum foil, and freeze part of the cake for later.

RUTH'S HONEY CAKE

Survivor | **RUTH WEBBER**

YIELDS 2 LOAVES

½ cup vegetable oil, plus more for greasing the pans
1½ cups honey
1 cup strong brewed coffee
½ cup dried cherries, cut into small pieces (If you don't have cherries, you use something else and improvise. What can I tell you!)
3 tablespoons brandy
½ cup sliced almonds
3½ cups plus 1–2 teaspoons all-purpose flour
1¼ cups packed brown sugar
4 eggs
1 teaspoon baking powder
1 teaspoon baking soda
¼ teaspoon salt
¼ teaspoon ground cloves
½ teaspoon ground ginger
¼ teaspoon ground nutmeg
1 teaspoon ground cinnamon
1 tablespoon orange zest

Preheat the oven to 325°F. Grease two 5-by-9-inch loaf pans and line them with wax paper, then grease the paper.

In a saucepan, bring the honey and coffee to a boil; set aside to cool.

Soak the dried cherries in the brandy for about 30 minutes, then drain. In a small bowl, mix the almonds and cherries with 1 to 2 teaspoons flour to coat (this prevents them from sinking to the bottom of the cake).

In the bowl of an electric mixer, blend ½ cup oil, sugar, and eggs. In a separate bowl, combine the remaining 3½ cups flour, baking powder, baking soda, salt, cloves, ginger, nutmeg, and cinnamon. Stir the dry ingredients into the mixer alternately with the coffee mixture until smooth. Fold in the almond-cherry mixture and orange zest.

Pour the batter into the prepared loaf pans and bake for 1 hour 10 minutes, or until a rich golden brown. Do not remove. Turn off the oven and leave the cakes in the oven to gradually cool for at least 10 minutes, to prevent them from caving. Cool, slice, and serve.

Note: Continue the cooling for another 15 minutes out of the oven. Run a knife around the inside of the pan, then put a plate over the pan and flip it over. Wrap in plastic and refrigerate. Bring out of the refrigerator and let come to room temperature before slicing and serving.

INDEX

ACKNOWLEDGMENTS

To Auschwitz-Birkenau survivors and their families who have generously shared their memories, time, and help: all that this book is, we owe to you. We are also immensely grateful to five Auschwitz-Birkenau survivors who joined us in person at a special photoshoot in New York City in October 2021: Michael Bornstein, Lois Flamholz, Tova Friedman, Eugene Ginter, and David Marks.

A very special acknowledgment goes out to Ronald S. Lauder, the Chairman of the Auschwitz-Birkenau Memorial Foundation. Thanks to his invaluable and continued support, enthusiasm, as well as his conviction and commitment to this project, we were able to turn a vision into reality during a very challenging time of a global pandemic.

Additional gratitude goes to the generous and inspirational Jo Carole Lauder for her encouragement and suggestions. Thanks to Mrs. Lauder's ideas and help, we get to include Elie Wiesel's family latkes recipe in this volume.

Thanks to the excellent staff of the Auschwitz-Birkenau Memorial Foundation, who worked on this project, interviewed the survivors and their families, collected handwritten notes and vintage photographs, assisted during the photoshoot, and communicated with the survivors in the most thoughtful way. We are also thankful for the advice and support of the Board of our Foundation and Jackie Scalisi. A great thanks to the Director of the Auschwitz-Birkenau Museum and Memorial, Piotr M.A. Cywiński, who provided encouragement for this project and contributed to the volume.

We are so grateful to Chris Steighner and the incredible and supportive team at Melcher Media. They have generously helped us navigate the nuances of the publishing world from the very beginning and have continued to share their passion, positivity, and encouragement. It has been such a pleasure to work with them.

We are indebted to Ellen Silverman, whose photographs brought life to the stories and memories shared by survivors. Ellen has gone above and beyond to ensure that this volume is beautiful, elegant, and inviting. She also extended a tremendous warmth and joy to the survivors who came to our photoshoot.

We were also thrilled to have an immensely talented creative team: Christine Albano, who beautifully styled all the dishes; prop stylist Suzie Myers; and Roberto de Vicq de Cumptich, who worked hard to ensure that the book is beautiful from cover to cover.

A very special thanks to all of our friends, who—behind the scenes—have tested the recipes, provided feedback on the manuscript, and offered guidance on all the aspects of this project: Gosia Szymanska-Weiss, Krystyna Zalewska, Sara Bakerman, and Josh Kazdin.

HONEY CAKE & LATKES

www.preserveauschwitz.org
Printed in China
ISBN: 978-1-59591-123-0
10 9 8 7 6 5 4 3

The survivors pictured in the contemporary photographs throughout the book are as follows:

2–3: Eugene Ginter; 26–27: Lois Flamholz and Michael Bornstein; 50: Eugene Ginter; 56–57: Tova Friedman and Eugene Ginter; 80, 84–85: David Marks; 114–115: Lois Flamholz; 140–141: Tova Friedman; 150: Lois Flamholz; 164–165: Michael Bornstein; 175: Tova Friedman and Eugene Ginter; 179: Tova Friedman; 187: Michael Bornstein.

All vintage photographs on pages xii–xvii are courtesy of the survivors who contributed recipes to this book.

This book was produced by
Melcher Media, Inc.

124 West 13th Street
New York, NY 10011
www.melcher.com

Founder and CEO: *Charles Melcher*
Vice President and COO: *Bonnie Eldon*
Editorial Director: *Lauren Nathan*
Production Director: *Susan Lynch*
Executive Editor: *Christopher Steighner*
Senior Editor: *Megan Worman*

Photographer: *Ellen Silverman*
Photo Assistant: *Arien Chang Castan*
Food Stylist: *Christine Albano*
Food Stylist Assistant: *Dylan Going*
Prop Stylist: *Suzie Myers*
Prop Stylist Assistant: *Lauren Ringer*
Designer: *Roberto de Vicq de Cumptich*

Melcher Media would also like to acknowledge the contributions of Renee Bollier, Madison Brown, Natalie Danford, Cathy Dorsey, Shannon Fanuko, Luke Gernert, Carlie Houser, Grzegorz Jarzynowski (who created the artwork on the endpapers), Noa Lin, Elisabeth March, Match Pewter (who supplied the candlesticks on the cover, Match1995.com), Carolyn Merriman, Jennifer Milne, and Sarah Scheffel.